JobThink ™

to contribute to job and corporate performance

The *Exemplary Worker* Book Series

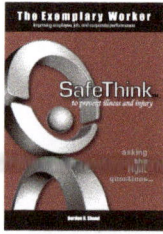

SafeThink™ ...to prevent illness and injury

SafeThink is a structured critical thinking strategy you can use to identify, predict, and control hazardous situations before, during, and after completing work. This cognitive-based safety strategy can be used on the fly, at work, at home, at play, and while driving. *SafeThink* also provides strategies for you to remain focused on your tasks.

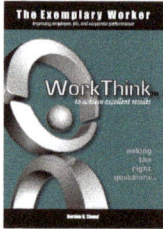

WorkThink™ ...to achieve excellent results

WorkThink is a thinking strategy you can use to achieve quality results with the least amount of effort. It usually takes little extra effort to do quality work instead of inferior work. *WorkThink* also emphasizes understanding the expectations of your supervisor, team leader, and customers so that you can achieve the excellent results they expect.

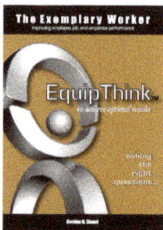

EquipThink™ ...to achieve optimal results

EquipThink is a thinking strategy for you to use tools, mobile equipment, and stationary equipment effectively and efficiently. The goals are for you to achieve the desired results with minimal stress on equipment, to conserve energy, and to extend equipment life. The input–process–output thinking strategy, in conjunction with identifying critical variables, is used to achieve optimal results.

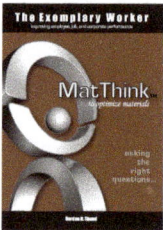

MatThink™ ...to optimize materials

MatThink is a thinking strategy you can use to make the most effective use of materials. The thinking strategy applies to recovering, processing, modifying, applying, transporting, and storing materials. Because equipment and materials are usually closely related, the input–process–output thinking strategy, in conjunction with identifying critical variables, is used to optimize material recovery and use.

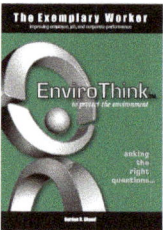

EnviroThink™ ...to protect the environment

Both industry and individuals have a responsibility to protect the environment. *EnviroThink* is a critical thinking strategy you can use to identify and respond to environmental issues for any job position that you might hold. *EnviroThink* helps you think through your work by asking yourself specific questions relating to environmental issues important to organizations.

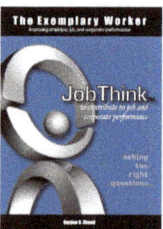

JobThink™ ...to contribute to job and corporate performance

Exemplary workers understand what is important to their organizations. They know the issues critical to business success and where to focus their efforts. *JobThink* addresses the critical thinking strategies you can use to identify what is important for job and corporate performance.

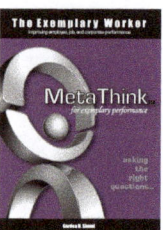

MetaThink™ ...for exemplary performance

MetaThink applies some of the thinking strategies addressed in previous books in different ways and also addresses new thinking strategies useful for the workplace. You can use these thinking strategies, along with the detailed thinking strategies addressed in other books of this series, to achieve exemplary performance.

The Exemplary Worker Book Series

"Rarely can workers from any sector access self-paced instructional materials that are easy-to-use, step-by-step guides to workplace learning. *The Exemplary Worker* book set is an exception. These books offer a good breadth of learning for workers in contexts ranging from: exemplary performance; job and corporate performance; results optimization; and work excellence. With meticulous organization, these essential training references are helpful guides for workers seeking to improve their performance. With prefaces designed to help trainers/instructors assist workplace learners, these books use critical thinking strategies that identify what matters to workers and supervisors considering people, equipment, materials, environments, and organization in concert."

—**Eugene G. Kowch, Ph.D.**, Leading Complex and Adaptive Learning Systems/Organizations, University of Calgary, Canada

"The power of thinking in determining our safety, health, and welfare is obvious, but how to manage such cognition or self-talk for injury prevention, self-motivation, and self-improvement is not so obvious. Answers are provided in this action-focused series of self-help books on *The Exemplary Worker* by Gordon D. Shand. He offers much practical information for leadership, safety, and well-being. Each of these books provides critical and structured thinking strategies for optimizing performance on several fronts, from improving safety and productivity in the workplace to actively caring as a teacher, parent, or friend."

—**E. Scott Geller, Ph.D.**, author of The Psychology of Safety Handbook; Alumni Distinguished Professor, Virginia Tech; Senior Partner, Safety Performance Solutions

"These are very practical books. I, myself, have been interested in the fundamental processes of human thinking. For creativity there is Lateral Thinking. For exploration there is the parallel thinking of the Six Thinking Hats. For perception there is the CoRT school programme. *The Exemplary Worker* series of books provide frameworks for focused thinking about specific situations. The frameworks guide the thinker to deal with the situation instead of messing about. That is why the books are so practical."

—**Dr. Edward de Bono**, Author of Lateral Thinking and Six Thinking Hats and creator of CoRT

The Exemplary Worker Book Series

JobThink ™

to contribute to job and corporate performance

Gordon D. Shand

HDC Human Development Consultants Ltd.
PO Box 4710, Edmonton, AB, Canada T6E 5G5
www.hdc.ca
www.safethink.ca

JobThink™

Library and Archives Canada Cataloguing in Publication
Shand, Gordon D.
    JobThink to contribute to job and corporate performance / Gordon
D. Shand.
(The exemplary worker book series)
ISBN 978-1-55338-053-5
    1. Work. 2. Performance. 3. Critical thinking. 4. Organizational
effectiveness. I. HDC Human Development Consultants II. Title.
III. Series: Exemplary worker
HD56.S52 2014   658.4'01   C2014-902763-4

Published by HDC Human Development Consultants Ltd.

Published in Canada

HDC *Human Development Consultants Ltd.*

Website: www.hdc.ca
E-mail: hdc@hdc.ca
Phone: (780) 463-3909

Acknowledgements

Developing *The Exemplary Worker* book series has been challenging and rewarding. I am certainly grateful for all the help I have received to produce quality products. Over one hundred people have contributed to the quality of the content and presentation.

Generally, I developed the first draft of the books working on evenings and weekends. I would blitz the first draft for a book—I produced the draft in a month to three months. During those times, my family's gracious support allowed me to concentrate on the task and to dialogue with them about the concepts. Once a first draft was produced, consultants in my firm carried out several edits as time allowed. HDC's Production Department developed illustrations and formats to produce a book ready for validation by industry. Because the people from industry volunteered their time and some validations were conducted in sequence, the validation process for each book took up to six months or more.

Many staff contributed to the development process. I would like to acknowledge those consultants who struggled to gather relevant content when working with customers—they gave cause to identify the thinking strategies used by exemplary workers and to develop the training for HDC consultants. Many thanks to the consultants who worked so diligently with me to produce the books. They were adamant in adhering to our standards for quality, even when I was burned out and wanted to put closure to a topic. Thanks to Janelle Beblow, Art Deane, Alice Graham, Jean MacGregor, and Bruno Schoenfelder for the wonderful edits and feedback. Thanks to Phil Jenkins, Kris Vasey, and Denise Hodgins for developing the illustrations, formatting the documents, and creating the book covers. Thanks to Maria Peck for coordinating the validations and field tests and proofing text. Their personal support, commitment to quality, and attention to detail are greatly appreciated.

I have been exceptionally fortunate to work with so many wonderful people from industry. They have been great mentors—they have made many contributions to my personal growth. A special thanks to nearly a hundred people who have volunteered their time to validate and field test the strategies.

Who is *The Exemplary Worker* series for?

The Exemplary Worker series benefits:

- **Individuals** who want to have outstanding performance
- **Apprentices and students** who want to work safely and effectively
- **Supervisors** who want staff to be more effective
- **Trainers** who want to contribute to improved corporate, job, and employee performance
- **Trades and technology instructors** who want their apprentices and students to work safely and effectively
- **Instructional designers** who want to ensure that training is relevant, useful, and practical
- **HR managers** who want to improve the development and retention of exemplary workers
- **Operations staff** who want to optimize production and minimize losses

Contents

JobThink™

Table of Contents (continued)

Table of Contents (continued)

JobThink™

Table of Contents (continued)

Preface

In addition to being skilled, exemplary workers use a broad range of *critical thinking strategies* to maintain outstanding performance. Exemplary workers know what is important to their jobs and organizations—they put their efforts in the right places by doing the most important things, doing them effectively, and doing them efficiently. Because they know what is important to the job and the organization, they effectively coordinate their actions with others and make decisions in the best interest of their organizations. Knowledge and thinking skills empower workers to achieve exemplary performance, be flexible as workplaces continue to evolve, and provide leadership within the workplace.

Exemplary performance can have many benefits for you, the line worker, lead operator, foreman, or supervisor, including:
- increased job satisfaction
- being recognized by your peers and supervisors as an effective employee
- increased potential for keeping your job during slow economic times
- increased potential for receiving salary/wage increases or bonuses
- increased opportunity for new or different work assignments
- increased potential for promotion

Each of the seven books in *The Exemplary Worker* series focuses on one of five domains (**PEMEO**):
- **P**eople
- **E**quipment
- **M**aterials
- **E**nvironment
- **O**rganization

Loss and/or optimization (LO) are the main themes for the domains, creating the word **LO-PEMEO™**. LO-PEMEO stands for Loss and Optimization of People, Equipment, Materials, Environment, and Organization. As an example: **L**oss to **P**eople is illness and injury; **O**ptimizing **P**eoples' performance is working effectively and efficiently; **L**oss to **E**quipment is damage and shortened operating life; and **O**ptimizing **E**quipment is using equipment effectively and efficiently. The books place a strong emphasis on using **thinking strategies** and **asking quality questions**—the goals are to minimize losses and optimize performance of PEMEO.

The series of books addresses both loss and optimization of each domain. We recommend that you complete each of the first six books in the sequence. However, the books can be studied in any order without difficulty. The last book in the sequence, *MetaThink*, should be read last. *MetaThink* applies some of the thinking strategies addressed in previous books but in different ways and also addresses new thinking strategies useful for the workplace.

Introduction to *The Exemplary Worker* Series

Over the last twenty-five years, the process of discovering *what's important* for exemplary worker performance has gone full circle. The process began for me when I interviewed exemplary workers to identify relevant training content. My premise was that exemplary workers know what is important for people to do their jobs effectively. Over time, it became apparent to me that one of the reasons exemplary workers perform so well is that they use a set of generic thinking strategies. After starting a consulting firm to design and develop training, I developed a comprehensive internal training program for our consultants and technical writers who develop training programs. The training focused on using generic thinking strategies and critical questions to identify training content that helps workers perform effectively. With a lot of support, I have revised our consultant training program and made it available to the public for people to learn and refine their personal thinking strategies to be exemplary workers.

The Exemplary Worker books are presented as a series. The same concepts underlie all seven books. For example, a safety incident may cause harm to a person and result in other losses—work may be suspended, equipment and materials damaged, the environment harmed. The organization could also experience unpredicted costs and have its reputation harmed. This introduction provides a framework and the key concepts that apply to the series. The discovery process and happenstances that led to the development of *The Exemplary Worker* series are explained to provide a setting and context to give meaning to the underlying concepts.

The Discovery Process

For me, the real discovery process began in 1985 when I founded the consulting firm HDC Human Development Consultants Ltd. (HDC) to design and develop customized technical training programs. I believed that it was possible to develop quality training for any industry without having an in-depth understanding of the organization, its technology, or the tasks that its people perform. The premise was that a well-thought-out instructional design and development process combined with effective consulting skills would be sufficient.

As founder of the company, I felt that I was successful in providing leadership to identify training content important to my customers—customers often asked me to do additional work. If I could do the work well, then certainly others in the firm could as well and, for some deliverables, do better.

The Plan

The plan was that I would work with customers to develop the outline of the training program (curriculum) and identify critical content for the program. The training program would be documented in one of three ways:
- a list of specific courses
- a list of general training objectives
- a competency-based training profile

Competency-Based Training Profile

The following illustration is a *partial* example of a competency-based training profile. The profile is a visual presentation of the competencies (tasks and support knowledge) that specific work groups require to do their work safely and effectively.

ORIENTATION	Complete Company Orientation	Describe Roles and Responsibilities	Identify Local Structures and Facilities	Describe and Use Communication Systems	Identify Customers and their Expectations
SAFETY	Describe and Use Personal Safety Equipment	Review Safety Handbook	Complete First Aid Training	Decribe and Operate Personal Gas Monitors	Describe Codes of Practice
ENVIRONMENT	Describe Environmental Responsibilities	Describe and Store Hazardous Wastes	Describe and Monitor Gas Emissions	Take Waste Water Samples	Describe and Participate in Spill Response Exercises
GENERAL KNOWLEDGE AND SKILLS	Describe Flammable Gas Measurements	Use Portable Multi-Gas Monitor	Describe Reciprocating Compressors	Prepare Maintenance Requests	
ROUTINE TASKS	Carry out Routine Equipment Checks	Change Process Filters	Describe and Change Corrosion Coupons	Monitor and Adjust Inhibitor Injection	Perform Housekeeping
SITE-SPECIFIC KNOWLEDGE AND TASKS	Describe Remore Process	Start and Adjust Remore Process	Describe and Change Remore Output Parameters	Perform Emergency Shutdown of Remore Process	Shut down Remore Process for Maintenance

Critical content for each competency is a list of the key issues a buddy or supervisor would emphasize when coaching the trainee. The end product is a *scope document* listing the key issues and ensuring continuity between competencies—no overlaps or gaps in content. As an example of a scope document, here is a partial list of key issues for the competency *Purge Piping and Station Systems*:

- replacing one medium with another to prevent combustible or toxic condition
- important to prevent:
  – people being exposed to toxic gases
  – possibility of a fire
- piping should only be purged after system has been opened and exposed to a foreign substance
- stations purged in preparation for startup
- some stations have automatic purging for specific piping and equipment
- automatic purging sequence must be checked
- always purge in direction gas migrates (up or down)
- criteria for length of time to purge include volume, pressure, and amount of connected equipment

In a profiling workshop, I used a brainstorming technique with four to sixteen of the customer's employees to identify competencies and critical content. The workshops were mentally demanding. On the one hand, I was concerned that the scope of training and performance requirements be limited and only address competencies and content that were considered important to the workers, their supervisors, and the organization. On the other hand, I was concerned that critical issues affecting people and the business were not overlooked. During these workshop sessions, I was constantly searching for relevant, useful, and practical content. What do the workers do? Is there a special way of doing the task? How do they know they are doing a good job? What can go wrong? How can the equipment be damaged or its life shortened? What do you mean by product quality? What about safety and the environment? Does the organization have special policies and ways of doing business? What is important and to whom or what? What questions should I be asking the group? I did not have a clear set of criteria or a structured thinking process that I could use to provide leadership in identifying training content that was important to the worker and the supervisor.

Working with Subject Matter Experts (SMEs)

I certainly believed that asking quality questions was more important than providing content. Answers to the questions could be provided by the customer's experienced employees. The term *subject matter experts* (*SME*s) is often used to refer to the organization's staff who provide content to training consultants and technical writers. Unfortunately, some SMEs, having in-depth knowledge of the tasks, technology, and the organization, had difficulties identifying content important for training. These SMEs expected consultants to provide leadership to identify relevant content. I soon discovered that my consultants often had difficulties in providing leadership to SMEs trying to identify content that was relevant, practical, and useful. When reviewing the first draft of training modules, information that would help trainees do their jobs more effectively, efficiently, and safely would often be missing. Nor would the supervisor's concerns always be addressed. Sometimes, information would be included that was of little value in helping workers do their jobs well and making decisions in the best interest of their organizations. When consultants asked me for direction as to the types of content that were relevant for training, I could not provide a comprehensive explanation. If the company was going to be successful in the future, I needed to find ways to define content that was relevant, practical, and useful—content that contributed to employee, job, and corporate performance.

Customer feedback gave me reason to believe that I was providing adequate leadership to identify relevant content; that I was asking quality questions. The truth of the matter was I did not have a formal list of types of question I should ask. In many ways, I was relying on intuition to ask the right questions. I needed to find a way to articulate a content gathering strategy that consultants could use with a variety of customers in different lines of business, different technologies, different hiring practices and performance expectations, and different ways of conducting business. I needed to find a way to identify the specific types of question consultants could ask SMEs to identify important training content—content that would help workers perform their jobs safely and effectively and contribute to meeting corporate objectives.

To help our training consultants and technical writers gain a better understanding of our customers, their businesses, goals, and concerns, I took consultants along to the competency-based profiling sessions. Listening to the group discussions and individual insights about the work and the business always provided learning beyond the information recorded in the program outline and scope document. This learning should be valuable when working with SMEs to identify detailed content for the training resources. Having this preliminary knowledge about the customer seemed to help some consultants be better at identifying relevant training content, but other consultants continued to struggle. I concluded that knowledge about the customer was valuable but didn't give consultants the strategies they needed to provide leadership when working with SMEs.

The Importance of Training Content Being Relevant to the Organization, Job, and Employees

Project reviews with customers were very useful for gaining ideas on how to improve services and products. Feedback from SMEs was that HDC consultants asked more questions than anyone they had ever worked with before. On the other hand, our consultants felt that they didn't ask enough questions because relevant information had been missed. The real issue was to ask fewer questions but more *quality* questions— questions that addressed issues that were important to employees, the job, and the organization. Certainly, customers strongly indicated that identifying relevant, useful, and practical content was the most important quality concern they had regarding the development of training resources. Customers also were adamant that consultants provide direction and leadership when working with SMEs to identify relevant content.

At the close of each project, I would ask the customer what additional training might be useful for consultants to help them be more effective at identifying relevant content. Suggestions included that consultants could increase their technical knowledge, or have a better understanding about safety management systems, environment management systems, or management styles. In response to suggestions, we began providing additional internal training using off-the-shelf technical training materials when possible. The additional training helped consultants to better understand what SMEs were telling them but only resulted in marginal improvements in consultants being able to provide leadership to identify relevant content. I concluded that the knowledge is useful but not sufficient in helping consultants (and workers) to identify issues important to employee, job, and corporate performance.

To compound the problem of identifying relevant content, expectations in industry were changing from developing entry level training (do as I tell and show you and don't ask why) to exemplary level training (maximizing productivity and making quality decisions) and every level between those two extremes. These changing expectations created difficulties in determining the content and amount of detail to include in training and keeping within training development budgets. Customers were upset if training materials included content they did not want and were not willing to pay for. Customers could also be disappointed if the training did not include content that they considered important. In many ways, the concerns consultants had in understanding the customer's expectations are the same concerns an employee new to a job would have.

When I had worked with exemplary workers, I discovered that one of their strategies was to confirm expectations. So we used the same strategy and built more confirmation checks into the development process to ensure the content was what customers wanted. Unfortunately, the confirmation checks were good at confirming that the documented content was what customers wanted but did not effectively address concerns about omissions of content important to customers (e.g., safety, equipment life).

Identifying Thinking Strategies Used by Exemplary Workers

Developing internal training for consultants to effectively identify relevant, useful, and practical content proved to be very difficult. Having consultants participate in the profiling sessions to learn about the customer, developing scope documents, providing technical and organization training, and building in confirmation checks had some value but weren't sufficient in helping them to provide leadership to identify relevant training content.

The instructional systems design models I was familiar with generally placed a strong emphasis on instructional development processes and only provided marginal direction and strategies on how to provide leadership to identify content that was important to customers. Certainly, the design of instruction and the nature of the content had an effect on each other. I suspected that there were instructional designs in which generic module structures and generic types of content would work for some types of technology and associated training outcomes. It would be several more years, after we had a large inventory of customized self-instructional modules, before we were able to develop a set of generic boilerplates (list of section and sub-section titles) for specific technologies and training outcomes. These *boilerplates* provided general structures for self-instruction and listed the types of content that *could* be included (but not necessarily included) in each section. No doubt, the SMEs that I worked with had mentally created their own boilerplates to be effective when working with specific types of equipment.

My initial effort to develop training to identify relevant content proved to be fairly impractical. Fortunately, several events provided me with the fundamental concepts needed to develop strategies that consultants could use to identify relevant content.

One of HDC's customers had a very demanding supervisor who was exceptionally analytical. In fact, he was by far the most powerful analytical thinker I have met. He was also driven to prevent anything negative from happening. He would always be analyzing situations and wanted to know all the *hows* and *whys* about every aspect of the instructional design that came to mind. Once a week I would make a personal visit to address his concerns. On one of those visits, he demanded to know what type of content should be addressed in the training. He said he asked our consultant the same question and the consultant's response was that *he would write self-instruction on anything as long as we told him the content*. Obviously, the consultant was not providing leadership when working with the SME to identify training content that would help the operators perform their work safely and effectively. For me, it was confirmation that our internal training was not very effective in helping our consultants to provide leadership.

My immediate response to his demand was to give some general criteria for identifying relevant content. *Well, safety, environment, equipment life, product quality, and customer satisfaction are important. Adhering to legislation and making decisions are important, too.*

There was a long silence—a lot of mental processing was going on in his head. Finally, he nodded and said, *Good. Let's tell the consultant and the senior operator what you just said.* The bottom line for this customer was that the training we were developing would contribute to his staff doing their work effectively and safely and making good decisions.

The interaction I had with that customer was the moment of discovery for me! The three-hour drive back to the office gave me time to reflect on what had just happened. Obviously, until I was asked, I had not been able to see the forest for the trees. Ask any business person what is important to their business success and he or she would give a list of areas of concern similar to the one I gave to my customer. No doubt the business person's list would be more extensive and include additional concerns affecting productivity and controlling losses—all businesses want to get the most out of their assets, including their people. Businesses prefer to have exemplary workers, workers that contribute to business success. Certainly, the training we develop for customers must help workers be effective in doing their jobs.

Creating the LO-PEMEO Model to Identify Relevant Training

I reflected on the thinking process I was using to identify relevant content when developing training profiles and scope documents. The questions that I had been asking myself during the sessions addressed the optimization and prevention of losses primarily to People, Equipment, Materials, Environment, and the Organization as a whole. Surely, the questions would take on meaning when the work environment was considered. And one way of assessing the work environment was to consider the conditions, actions, and events within the workplace that affect PEMEO.

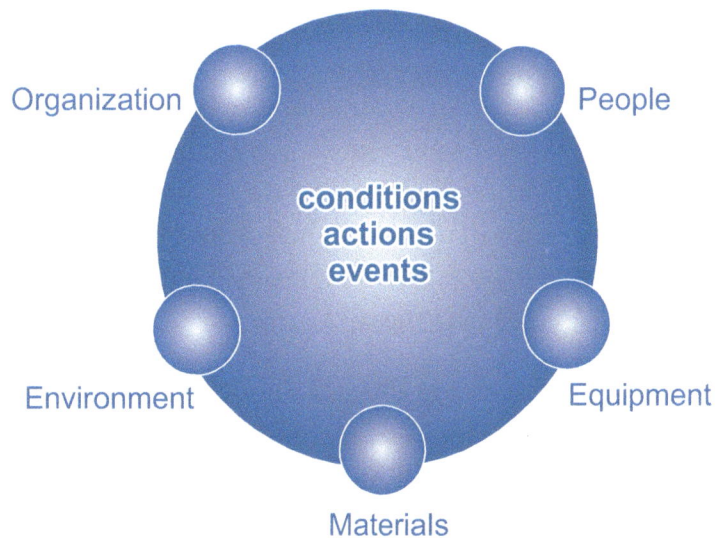

Most exciting for me, I could combine the concepts of optimization and controlling losses of organizational assets such as people and equipment to create a model and strategy for identifying relevant content. The LO-PEMEO model was born. Each of the five domains (people, equipment, materials, etc.) shown in the above illustration had potential for optimization and loss. An example of loss to people is illness and injury. Loss of materials when processing ore is the inefficient recovery of the desired products. Optimization of materials in construction is to use the right materials and maximize the use of the materials. The following illustration shows the combinations of loss and optimization of PEMEO.

LOSS					OPTIMIZATION
Loss: People	LP	P	OP	Optimization:	People
Loss: Equipment	LE	E	OE	Optimization:	Equipment
Loss: Materials	LM	M	OM	Optimization:	Materials
Loss: Environment	LE	E	OE	Optimization:	Environment
Loss: Organization	LO	O	OO	Optimization:	Organization

Exemplary workers consider the potential for Loss and Optimization of each domain of PEMEO (i.e., LO-PEMEO) while they work. So LO-PEMEO was used as the framework and structure for *The Exemplary Worker* series of books. For example, loss to people (LP) is safety—the book *SafeThink* focuses on using a structured critical thinking strategy to identify and predict hazardous situations to prevent illness and injury.

Interestingly, several years later, I was introduced to a loss control model created by Frank E. Bird that used PEME as an acronym. I have always wondered if it would have saved me a lot of effort if I had known of Bird's loss control model earlier. Or would that knowledge have put in place constraints such that I would never have created the LO-PEMEO model?

While driving back to my office, I thought about how fortunate I had been over the years to work with a lot of exemplary performers, many of them my SMEs. Our customers gave us SMEs who are exemplary workers because the belief is that exemplary workers know what is important for business success and will provide training content that is relevant to corporate, job, and employee performance. When I had asked the SMEs if there were any concerns about issues such as safety, equipment, or materials, they would often look at the ceiling and ponder for a while. If they said yes, they would go on and give me further clarification. If they said no, I would continue to ask different questions. When I thought about it, the questions that I asked SMEs usually focused on concerns about LO-PEMEO. I always wondered what the SMEs were thinking when they were looking at the ceiling and pondering the answers to my questions. Eventually, I asked them. Interestingly, different SMEs from different companies and lines of business had similar concerns. For example, damage to equipment often involved shock from a sudden change in physical forces or temperature. The sources for causing damage could be people, material, or any of the other three domains. In fact, *each domain has the potential to affect the other domains.* Whether the SMEs were aware of it or not, they were mentally searching for specific workplace concerns relating to LO-PEMEO. In many ways, even at the detailed level, *the thinking strategies of exemplary workers were similar and generic.* Certainly, being aware of one's own thinking strategies contributes to planning and working effectively and helps to communicate effectively when collaborating with others and mentoring apprentices.

Linking Corporate, Job, and Employee Performance

When organizations develop standards, procedures, and training, they want to realize an improvement in corporate performance. Improving *corporate performance* is often achieved by either filling a gap in performance or by preparing the organization to move towards new goals. The following illustration lists some criteria that can be used to measure corporate performance.

PERFORMANCE REPORT

Customer Satisfaction	UP
Production	UP
Product Quality	UP
Equipment Run Time	UP
Equipment Damage	DOWN
Energy Consumption	DOWN
Material Waste	DOWN
Personal Injuries	DOWN
Maintenance Costs	DOWN
Environment Damage	DOWN
Rework Time	DOWN

At the operational or job level, the supervisor also has concerns about performance. Within his or her roles, responsibilities, and authority, the supervisor is expected to maximize productivity and minimize losses. Improved *job performance* contributes to improved corporate performance. The supervisor therefore represents the concerns and goals of the organization and must use specific resources and assets (including people) to effectively achieve the goals. The supervisor must also be able to motivate, coordinate, and assign staff to effectively carry out the work. Furthermore, worker performance affects job performance which, in turn, affects corporate performance.

Employee performance affects business results. Employees are expected to work effectively and efficiently and make good use of materials and technology. Expectations of performance are articulated to line employees both orally and in writing. In turn, employees have concerns about understanding the expectations and working safely, effectively, and efficiently to meet the expectations. The following illustration is of a person new to a job asking questions relating to corporate, job, and employee performance issues.

What's important to the business?

What does the team leader expect of me?

What am I supposed to do?

How am I supposed to do it?

How do I know I've done well?

How does my work affect others?

Is there a better way?

What tools and equipment are used?

Could I get hurt?

Could I injure others?

Could I damage the equipment?

Does this product affect the environment?

How much waste is acceptable?

How can I prevent...?

Will the customer be satisfied?

What should I do if ...?

What would happen if ...?

Do I have the authority to take action?

What action?

Whom should I inform?

What does ...?

How does ...?

What caused ...?

What is the reason?

What are the consequences for ...?

What questions should I be asking?

What answers do I need?

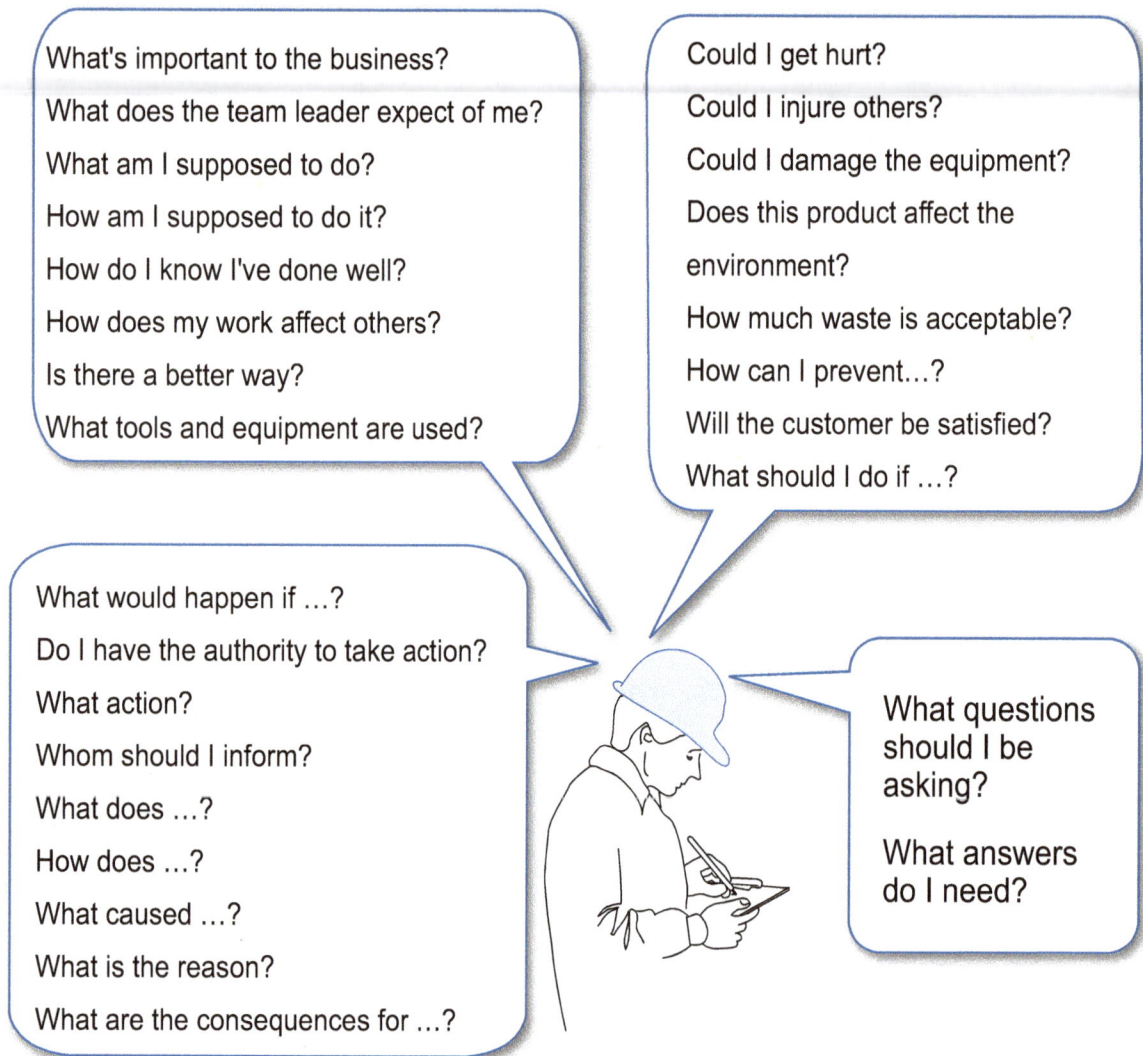

Many of the questions are generated by the LO-PEMEO strategy and focus on performance:
- What is important?
- What are the issues?
- What questions should I ask?

The person new to the job needs answers to the questions in the illustration to quickly learn to do that job effectively and efficiently. Interestingly, two employees with similar experiences and skills who are new to a job can perform quite differently. One employee will be uncertain about the work and become stressed if work conditions change. The other employee will initiate actions and make good work-related decisions for the organization within a few weeks. One of the factors that makes the difference in performance between the two employees is the knowledge about what is important to job and corporate performance. Understanding *what is important* provides criteria for focusing one's efforts and for making decisions. LO-PEMEO is a good start in identifying what is important to the organization. Although many of the issues identified by LO-PEMEO are generic, each organization has its own business strategies, resources, and priorities. As such, each organization could place a different emphasis on each issue identified by LO-PEMEO. And that's why asking the *right* questions is so valuable. Questions focus on key issues; the answers to the questions are unique to the organization, workplace, and specific circumstances. *The Exemplary Worker* series provides many of the questions that workers need to ask of themselves and of others to achieve exemplary performance.

Understanding Organizations for Exemplary Worker Performance

Exemplary workers understand what is important to the organization so that they put their efforts in the right places, do the right things, and make good decisions in the best interests of their organizations. For workers to have exemplary performance, they need to have an understanding of organizations in general, and a specific understanding of their own organization. Training and performance consultants also need to have a general understanding of organizations to be effective at developing customized training—training that is relevant, useful, practical, and reflects the organization for what it is. There is a lot of literature on organizations but most of it is more complex than training consultants need. Generally, the literature does not directly address issues important to designing and developing customized training for industry.

So, what issues are important? For consultants at HDC (and exemplary workers in other organizations) to be effective, they must be able to identify and understand organizational issues from different points of view. Imagine a roomful of statues facing in different directions. The room has many doors, each opened by a different work group or discipline. Each doorway has a different view of the statues.

For consultants to get a broader understanding of the organization, they need to view the statues from different doors. Ideally, consultants would walk around the statues to get many different points of view. The consultant must be prepared to consider different points of view within a specific organization to be effective at understanding the organization and identifying issues important to employee, job, and corporate performance.

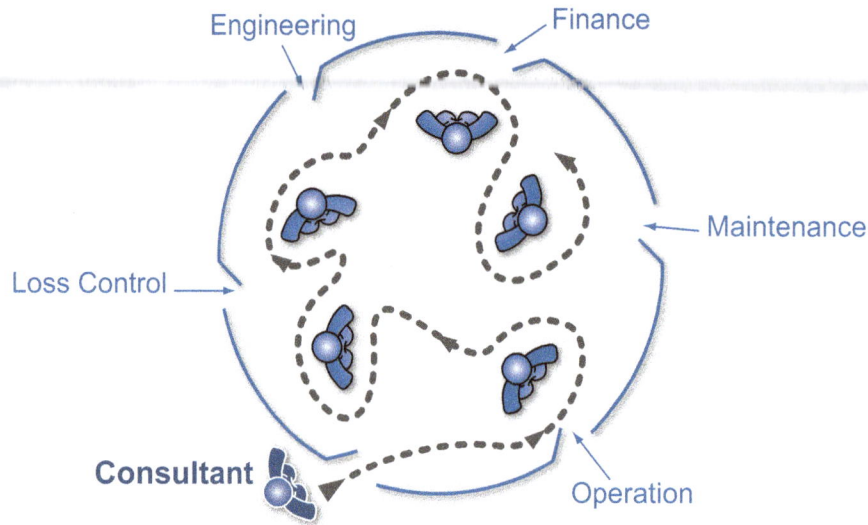

Both exemplary workers and training/performance consultants benefit from an understanding of relationships between business resources, organizational structure, business strategies, corporate objectives, and performance standards. Exemplary workers gain an understanding as to how their line of work fits into the organization as a whole. In doing so, they appreciate how their work affects others and they potentially make better use of organizational resources. This understanding about organizations also helps training consultants and technical writers to be more effective at designing and developing training that is customized, reflects the business, and has excellent value for the customer.

The approach I take with consultants to learn about organizations is to pretend to build a new business. Would the line of business be a service or a product? What is the mission? If the business is a service, then performing tasks is the main way to generate revenue and tools/equipment provide support for carrying out the work. If the line of business is to use technology to make products, then the technology dictates many of the tasks that workers must do. Having resources to achieve specific results is essential but not sufficient for business success. The resources must also be managed effectively. The following illustration identifies some key constituents of a business.

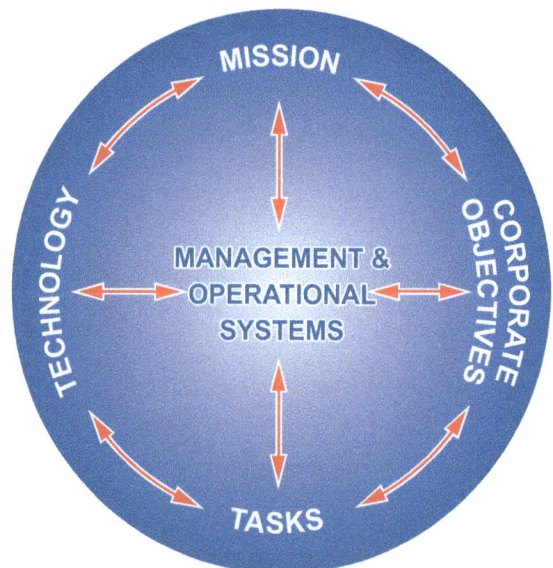

The book *JobThink* uses the previous model to provide a practical way for workers to understand organizations. This understanding helps workers to effectively focus their efforts and make decisions in the best interests of their organizations.

Of particular interest are the *corporate objectives*. Corporate objectives provide direction for using technology, performing tasks, and coordinating work to effectively achieve the corporate mission. The following table lists areas of concern, common to many organizations, for which corporate objectives may be developed.

Areas addressed by Corporate Objectives

- safety
- environment
- legislation
- equipment reliability and life
- equipment optimization
- energy use
- quality
- waste control
- loss control
- cost control
- customer satisfaction
- public image
- public disruption
- reputation
- communication
- teamwork

For a specific organization, a list of corporate objectives can be generated by expanding the organization's strategic business objectives or by using LO-PEMEO. Some companies issue strategic business objectives to provide direction to employees as to where to put their energy and focus for business success. Strategic business objectives identify what the organization must do well to be successful. For example, leaders in an organization may believe that it is essential for business success to have reliable service and satisfied customers. Organizations may identify five to eight strategic objectives. Within a department, the list of objectives (or goals) may be expanded in more detail to address issues specific to the department's mandate.

The expanded list of corporate objectives can also be generated using LO-PEMEO— each of the items in the above table relates to one or more of the LO-PEMEO domains.

Corporate objectives are fundamental to exemplary performance because they define what is *important* to the organization, the job, and workers. Corporate objectives provide a ***formal link*** between organizational goals and worker performance. Workers can use corporate objectives as criteria for working effectively and efficiently and for making decisions in the best interest of their organizations. Training consultants and technical writers can use corporate objectives to identify relevant, useful, and practical training content. Refer to my book, *Interviewing to Gather Relevant Content for Training* for:

- information about applying critical thinking skills to identify relevant content for training
- an interviewing process that consultants and technical writers can use to interview SMEs to gather relevant content

Developing Training to Identify What is Important to Employee, Job, and Corporate Performance

With the LO-PEMEO and business models, I could now develop training for consultants to provide leadership to identify relevant content. The LO-PEMEO model was the most practical approach to use to structure the training because it relates directly to work and job issues. The organizational model can be integrated into the training on loss and optimization of organization, LO-O. For the training on these models to be useful, the training needs to be flexible and apply to a broad range of work, technology, and organizations. The training must also provide strategies for people to think through their work. That is what exemplary workers do—they think through their work. And, the thinking processes are generic so they apply to all types of industries, work environments, and jobs.

All of the training to identify relevant content is founded on using thinking strategies. An emphasis is placed on *concepts* and *generalities* to maintain a broad application of the thinking strategies. Furthermore, the thinking involves asking questions relating to LO-PEMEO. Asking questions is important to maintaining the broad application of the thinking strategies and helping people remain mentally engaged. Asking the *right* questions is often more important than finding the answers, because if the right questions are asked, answers can usually be found—answers that contribute to exemplary employee, job, and corporate performance.

Over several years, I developed training for all the combinations of LO-PEMEO. I also expanded the training to include consulting processes and a performance and training model to design, develop, and implement competency-based training and performance management systems. I was very fortunate to have excellent support from staff to edit and refine the training. HDC staff made important contributions to the training content and presentation. And, after the training resources were in use, we refined them further.

Developing *The Exemplary Worker* Series

After the HDC consultants' training resources had been used for ten years, I decided to go full circle and modify the resources for general use. A major rewrite was required; the new audience was very broad and the lines of work very diverse. The instructional design content had to be deleted. New and different examples of applying the thinking strategies were required for the books. To help the reader, each book required new learning activities. Exemplary workers in industry needed to field test and validate the content. Staff also needed to make major contributions to ensure the quality of each book. It took over six thousand hours to develop *The Exemplary Worker* series. In addition, industry has volunteered more than a thousand hours to field test and validate the content.

The Exemplary Worker series has many suggestions to help you not only be aware of your own thinking strategies but also help you to refine your strategies to achieve exemplary performance. You will also be better at mentoring others to perform better.

Gordon D. Shand
Edmonton, Alberta
Canada

Training Objectives

Upon completion of this book, you will be able to:

- Specify the constituents of your organization
- Describe the relationship between constituents
- Identify the resources used to achieve your organization's mission
- Define your organization's corporate and strategic business objectives and their functions
- Explain the impact of your work on other workers
- Identify the types of critical knowledge useful for most jobs
- Use a generic problem-solving model to solve work-related problems

Introduction

This book is one of *The Exemplary Worker* series of books. Books in the series all focus on using critical thinking strategies to identify ***what is important*** to employees, the job, and the organization. Each book focuses on one of five domains (**PEMEO**):

P   People

E   Equipment

M   Materials

E   Environment

O   Organization

Within each book, loss and/or optimization (LO) are the main themes, hence the word LO-PEMEO™:

Themes	Books
L-P Loss to People (Safety)	*SafeThink* Use a structured thinking strategy to identify and predict hazardous situations.
O-P Optimize People's Performance	*WorkThink* Work effectively and efficiently.
LO-E Loss and Optimization of Equipment	*EquipThink* Use tools and equipment effectively and efficiently.
LO-M Loss and Optimization of Materials	*MatThink* Use materials effectively and efficiently.
LO-E Loss and Optimization of the Environment	*EnviroThink* Protect the environment.
LO-O Loss and Optimization of the Organization	*JobThink* Contribute to job and corporate performance.
LO-PEMEO Use thinking strategies for the workplace	*MetaThink* Integrate thinking strategies for exemplary performance.

The fundamental premise of LO-PEMEO is to *ask questions*. By asking yourself questions, you remain alert. By seeking answers, you continually learn and become more effective in the workplace and adaptable to changes. The big question is: *What questions should I ask?* The questions identified in LO-PEMEO help you to ask many of the right questions to do your job effectively and efficiently with minimal effort.

When starting a new job position, people with similar education and experience can vary dramatically in their abilities to learn to do the work effectively. Some people quickly learn what is important to the organization. They soon begin making effective decisions and providing leadership to meet job and business goals. Others struggle to understand their jobs and provide leadership. These people may be very knowledgeable about the work but can become uncertain when work conditions change. They often do not know where to focus their efforts. People around them may be wary, particularly about safety. One key difference between these two types of people is their ability to recognize what is important to their organization.

When you understand your organization (the big picture) and what is important to your organization, you are able to:
- focus your efforts in ways that contribute to your job and to your organization's performance
- be effective at making the *right* decisions that are in the best interest of your organization.

Working in ways that contribute to job and corporate performance can have many benefits for you, including:
- being recognized by peers and supervisors as an effective employee
- increased potential for keeping your job during slow economic times
- increased potential for receiving salary/wage increases or bonuses
- increased opportunity for new or different work assignments
- increased potential for promotion
- increased job satisfaction

This book provides suggestions for you to work effectively within your organization, contributing to job and corporate performance. The book:
- identifies five constituents (components, parts) of an organization, describes the relationships of these constituents, and how the constituents affect your workplace performance
- identifies the resources that organizations use and describes how you can use these resources effectively
- describes an organization's strategic business objectives (SBOs), the strategies organizations use to achieve them, and how you can contribute to business success

- describes how the work you do impacts the work of other workers and departments and the need for workers and departments to effectively coordinate work
- describes ways for you to work thoughtfully to contribute to job and corporate performance
- provides a problem-solving model that you can use to resolve work-related problems

The learning activities that are integrated into this book provide you with opportunities to apply these critical thinking strategies to your job, workplace, and personal activities. Each learning activity relates to specific concepts addressed in this book. It is recommended that you complete each learning activity as you progress through the book. The Job Aid lists the key questions you need to ask and for which you need to seek answers to contribute effectively to job and corporate performance.

To effectively contribute to job and corporate performance, you need to ask and seek answers to a set of critical questions. Various sections of this book list *critical thinking* questions that you can ask yourself to determine what is important to the organization. Refer to the Job Aid which lists the critical thinking questions when doing the learning activities.

Because we assume that workers want to do their work well, be productive, and continually improve their performance, issues of attitude are not addressed.

Related Training Books

Three other books relating to people and their performance are:

SafeThink—focuses on a thinking strategy workers can use to identify potential hazardous situations.

WorkThink—focuses on performing tasks safely, effectively, and efficiently

MetaThink—an advanced book that focuses on thinking strategies that exemplary workers use to identify ways to optimize the use of resources, minimize losses, and contribute effectively to business performance.

Constituents of an Organization

There are many facets to an organization: culture, organizational structure, management strategies, assets, markets, and finance, to name a few. To work effectively and make *good* decisions, you need to understand your organization. A practical way of describing an organization is to break it into five constituents (components, parts). When you understand these five constituents and how they affect each other, you will be able to focus your efforts and make decisions in the best interest of your organization.

This section describes the five main constituents of an organization:
- mission
- tasks
- technology (tools, equipment, materials, processes)
- management and operational systems
- corporate objectives

At the end of this section, the constituents are presented graphically as a model to show their relationships to each other. Section 3 describes how these constituents interrelate and how this knowledge can help you be more effective at contributing to your job and your organization.

2.1 Mission

To effectively contribute to your organization, you need to have an understanding about your organization, what it is, what it does, and how it functions. Mission statements help define an organization and may specify its:

- line of business
- key business goals
- business strategies for achieving the goals
- key beliefs, values, and vision for conducting business

An organization's **line of business** is what the organization does, for example, maintain lawns, manufacture cars, sell real estate, construct homes. Many lines of business can be categorized into a group such as service, construction, or manufacturing. For example, a landscape maintenance company provides a service, a furniture builder manufactures a product.

The **mission** statement may also state the organization's long-term and/or annual **business goals**. For example:

- provide a healthy return to its owners or shareholders
- achieve asset growth
- increase revenue
- reduce operating costs
- increase profits
- expand market share
- diversify or rationalize the business (expand lines of business or limit lines of business)
- meet the increasing need of public services

Long-term goals help define what is important to the organization and provide some direction for exerting business effort and allocating resources. Short-term goals may be further defined with specific values or percentage change. For example:

- increase annual profit by 2 million dollars
- increase revenue by 30 million dollars this year
- increase productivity by 25 000 units in the fourth quarter
- reduce operating costs by 15% this year
- add 30 sales outlets nationally each year
- maintain the current level of public satisfaction at 95%

The numerical values are benchmarks for determining whether or not the goals have been achieved.

In some cases, short-term goals may not align with long-term goals. Sometimes, in the short term, an organization may have to alter its goals in response to change (e.g., a slowdown in the economy or an unforeseen tragedy such as a fire destroying a facility). To remain viable, an organization may have to reduce budgets targeted to achieve long-term goals.

The mission statement may also state the **business strategies** that have been chosen to achieve the goals. For example:
- produce products that are of exceptionally high quality (and price)
- use sophisticated technology
- use a small labor force
- use workers from local or visible minority groups
- maintain long-term customers
- use a team approach to manage and carry out work

A mission statement also emphasizes the key strategies, beliefs, values, and vision for the organization. For example:
- do business with integrity
- ensure the safety of workers and the public
- protect the environment

NOTE

Beliefs, values, and strategies are an important part of the culture of an organization.

LEARNING ACTIVITY 1

Identify your organization's mission

Understanding your organization's mission (the big picture) helps you focus your efforts to contribute to business success. Learning Activity 1 helps you to clarify how your job and department contribute to your organization's mission.

The *mission* statement provides the *biggest picture* of the organization. Some organizations use *business strategies, vision,* or *belief* statements, instead of a mission statement, to communicate the key aspects of the mission.

1a. Break down your organization's mission, business strategies, values, or belief statements into brief points.

_____

_____

_____

_____

_____

_____

1b. Select three of the points from 1a. For each point, explain how your job or the way you do your job supports the point. To think through this learning activity, you may find it helpful to first consider the consequences of **not** doing your job or **not** doing it well.

_____

_____

_____

_____

_____

_____

2.2 Tasks

A number of tasks must be performed to provide services or make products. Tasks with a common purpose may be grouped into specialties, such as operations or maintenance. Organizations with a large number of employees may form departments, such as operations, marketing, accounting, engineering, and health and safety. Within each of these departments, tasks may be grouped into subdivisions to meet specific needs and to coordinate the efforts of the work group. Titles, such as Lab Technician, Operator 5, or Mechanic 2, may be used to identify the position of workers who perform a specific group of tasks.

LEARNING ACTIVITY	2

Identify how tasks impact your organization's mission

This learning activity helps you understand the effects that the tasks you perform have on your organization's mission.

2.   List three tasks you perform that can have a significant effect on your organization's mission; explain the effect.

Task 1 _____

_____

Effect on mission _____

_____

_____

_____

_____

Task 2 _____

_____

Effect on mission _____

_____

_____

Task 3 _____

_____

Effect on mission _____

_____

Organizations often provide job descriptions to help people understand the scope of work they are expected to do (and, sometimes, what they are expected **not** to do). To contribute effectively to job and corporate performance, you not only need to understand the requirements of your job, you also need to understand:

- how your work impacts other people and other departments
- how the work of other people and other departments impacts your work

From one organization to the next, job descriptions can vary in the type of information provided, the level of detail, and the use of terms. The following definitions are used in this book. When possible, the terms have been listed from the most general to the most specific.

Discipline: A discipline is an area of specialization or study. The application of these specialized skills and knowledge relates to a set of jobs or occupations. Examples of disciplines include instrument technicians, gas plant operators, and industrial hygienists.

Job (broad definition): A job is what one does for a living. The term reflects the type of work one does and may be equivalent to one's occupation (e.g., electrician). The term *job* may be further defined to include the specific type of work or application of work. For example, an electrician may do only maintenance work or only new construction. A job consists of a set of duties; duties consist of a set of tasks.

Position: In an organization, a job may have more than one position. For example, a Gas Plant Operator (*job*) may work as the Inlet Operator (*position*) or as the Plant 5 Operator (*position*). A position exists, even if it is currently empty. For example, an organization may advertise for someone to fill the position of Site Trainer.

Roles: A role is a part played by someone in a workplace or organization, for example, the manager or team leader. Often a job encompasses more than one role. For example, a maintenance person works at a site as the maintenance person, a warehouseman, and a safety representative. In some cases, the person may fill only one role for a job. In this case the job title may suggest the job function or role, for example, the job of electronic repair technician may have only one role as an electronic repair person.

Responsibilities: Responsibilities are delegated and are often equated with duties. For example, a manager may be responsible for ensuring that vacation schedules are made and that annual performance reviews are carried out. The person who has been delegated specific responsibilities has an obligation to meet those expectations and is accountable if the expectations are not met.

Roles and Responsibilities: Job descriptions may have a section listing roles and responsibilities but do not make distinctions between roles and responsibilities. Roles and responsibilities statements help to define the scope and boundaries for the work.

Roles and responsibilities statements may identify your internal and external customers. Internal customers could be peers, a group within your department, or another department.

Duties: A duty is a subdivision of a job. A job usually includes several duties. Duties can be considered the major functions of the job. For example, a pipeline station operator's duties may include station operation, housekeeping, and minor maintenance. For a specific job, duties and responsibilities may be equivalent. A worker needs a specific set of knowledge, skills, behaviors, and attitudes to successfully complete his/her duties. A duty consists of a set of tasks.

Tasks: A task is a work activity that is part of a duty. A task has several features, including:
- a task can be assigned to one or more people
- a task has a beginning and an end
- a person doing a task can usually be observed
- the result of performing a task can often be measured (e.g., in terms of quality, quantity, time, and timeliness)

Examples of tasks are collecting water samples, monitoring equipment condition, starting compressor #5, removing old carpet from a house, and cooking hamburgers.

Job (narrow definition): The term job is often used to mean a specific work assignment or unit of work. The job has a beginning and an end, as in *When you have completed that* *job, come and see me.* An example of a job is installing a new roof on a building. A job often consists of several different tasks.

NOTE | This book uses the narrow definition of the term *job*.

Lines of Authority: In most organizations, each worker is normally directly accountable to only one person: the foreman, supervisor, team leader, or manager (i.e., the boss). That person delegates work and makes decisions in accordance with his or her limits of authority.

In large organizations, different departments have authority specific to that department's responsibilities. For specific issues, employees may have to communicate with departments other than their own (e.g., Health and Safety, Environment, Human Resources, or Accounting). Often, communication within and between departments is a critical issue that affects the efficiency and effectiveness of work and the organization.

Limits of Authority: Within each job position, a person is given some degree of authority to make decisions and take action. The specific authority that one is given depends on a number of factors, such as:

- The organizational structure that is in place can affect the scope or limits of authority for each job position. The organization may define the authority of each job position in general terms.
- The particular management style of the organization affects how decisions are made. For example, a self-directed team's decision-making process could require that all team members participate in the decision-making process rather than having one person make the decisions.
- The management style of the foreman, supervisor, team leader, or manager affects the type of decisions a worker can make. *Hands-on* leaders want to be informed and involved in making many of the decisions; other leaders prefer to delegate as much decision-making as possible without causing undue risk of losses.

- The person making the decisions and taking action may need specific qualifications or certifications, for example, satisfactory completion of site-specific training, certification as a tradesperson, professional engineer, or corrosion technologist.
- A person's competence and experience can also affect the degree of authority that is given. When people start in a new position, they may initially be given low risk, task-focused assignments. Over time, they may be given progressively more complex work assignments that require them to make more critical decisions.

Part of understanding the scope of work is to understand the expectations of performance: what has to be done, how it has to be done, and how well it has to be done. Knowing the desired quality and standards of performance are important to contributing to job and corporate performance. Sometimes, knowing the source of standards can provide incentive for meeting the standards when performing tasks. There are many sources of standards, including:

- ISO 9000 (quality)
- ISO 14000 (environment)
- legislated standards (e.g., for boiler and pressure vessels, welding, electrical, hoisting, fire detection and suppression, occupational health and safety)
- performance appraisals

For more information about standards of performance, refer to *WorkThink*.

The following partially completed illustration shows the relationship between corporate mission and the tasks that must be performed to achieve the mission. In the illustration, the tasks are not grouped into jobs or departments.

Note that in the sub-sections that follow, this illustration will be expanded to show the other constituents (technology, management and operational systems, and corporate objectives).

MISSION

TASKS

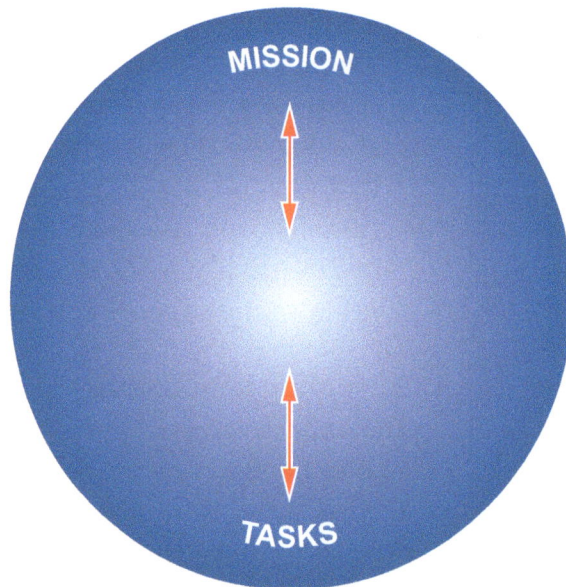

Specific tasks must be performed to achieve the mission.

LEARNING ACTIVITY	3

Define your roles and responsibilities

This learning activity focuses on how your job fits into your organization's structure.

3a. For your job position, list three major roles and responsibilities.

Job position _____

_____

Roles and responsibilities of your job position:

1. _____

2. _____

3. _____

3b. Identify your internal customers.

_____

_____

_____

3c.   Identify your external customers.

_____

_____

_____

3d.   Often, work groups within a department must coordinate work activities with work groups in other departments. The lines and limits of authority of each group must be defined to ensure the work objectives are effectively met. For example, in a pipeline operation, the Shipping Scheduler sets up product receipt and delivery schedules, the Maintenance Scheduler sets up equipment maintenance schedules, and the Control Center Operator (CCO) delivers products according to the schedules. If the CCO has to slow down or shut down the pipeline so that maintenance staff can make repairs, the Shipping Scheduler must change the schedule to cause minimal disruption for producers or customers. The timing of the equipment slowdown/shutdown may be a critical factor affecting customers and production.

If the CCO cannot make the deliveries as scheduled, the Shipping Scheduler must be informed so that he or she can change the shipping in ways that cause minimal disruptions for customers.

Identify a person, group, or department with which you must collaborate.

_____

3e.   State a work activity where you must collaborate with that person, group, or department.

_____

3f.   For that work activity, state your responsibility and the other person's, group's, or department's responsibility.

My responsibility is _____

_____

Other's responsibility _____

_____

3g. What are the negative effects on achieving the mission if the collaboration is not effective?

_____

_____

_____

2.3 Technology

Technology (equipment, tools, and materials) is one of the five main constituents of an organization. The technology an organization uses is dictated by the organization's line of business and the tasks the organization performs. There is a close relationship between technology and tasks:

- the tasks to be performed may determine the technology required to do the work
- the technology used may determine the tasks to be performed to operate and maintain the technology

In industries such as service and construction, the *tasks* to be performed and the specific *application* of the tasks dictate the specific technology to be used. For example, a company that builds roads uses heavy equipment, such as crawler tractors, and specific types and grades of road building materials, such as gravel or asphalt. An organization that installs materials (e.g., in buildings) uses tools designed for the specific type of materials being used (e.g., wood, steel, ceramic).

Manufacturing and processing materials often involve a major investment in equipment. The *technology* used for the various stages of manufacturing or processing determines many of the tasks that have to be performed.

In the following illustration, equipment and materials are grouped under the term technology.

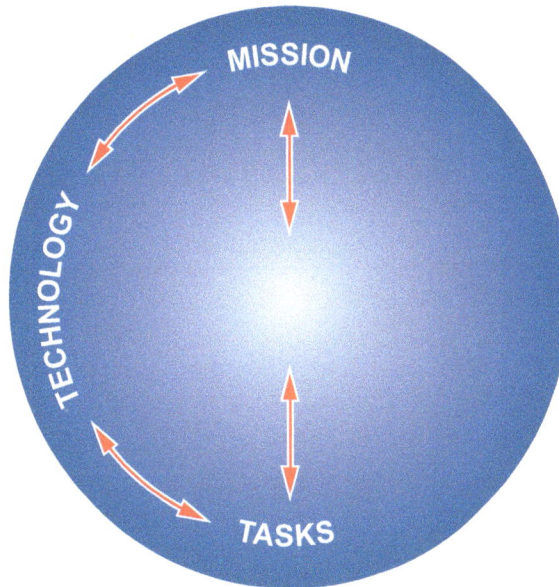

Relationship of technology and tasks to achieving mission

The relationship between the mission and the technology and tasks has many implications for an organization, including the initial capital investment to start the business and distribution of budgets to meet operating costs. The implications of these relationships are explained in more detail in Section 3.

<table>
<tr><td>**LEARNING ACTIVITY** **4**</td></tr>
</table>

Specify the relationship between technology, tasks, and mission

This learning activity requires you to determine whether your organization's line of business centers on:
- technology that dictates many of the tasks that need to be performed, or
- tasks that determine the type of technology required to carry out the tasks

4a. In your organization, specify whether the technology determines the tasks to be performed or the tasks determine the technology that needs to be used.

_____

_____

4b. Explain why you made that selection.

_____

_____

_____

_____

_____

2.4 Management and Operational Systems

Management and operational systems are needed to coordinate people and technology and provide direction to workers. In traditional organizations, supervisors plan, delegate, coordinate, monitor, control, and evaluate work and projects. In team environments, work teams carry out the traditional supervisory activities and related responsibilities.

At the job level, the organization's management has a major impact on employees and their work, including:
- defining roles, responsibilities, and the lines and limits of authority for each job position and/or team
- defining standards of performance and quality
- establishing methods of carrying out work including policies, practices, procedures, and the use of resources (e.g., equipment, materials, and people)
- defining employee selection criteria
- setting administrative protocols for carrying out work, communicating, decision-making, and reporting
- planning, coordinating, and assessing work
- administering payroll, benefits, and scheduling vacations

- setting up and using administrative system software and processes
- providing training relating to safety, the environment, and specific jobs

Management style affects how these decisions and activities are carried out. For example, management could make all the decisions or could consult with those who will be affected by the decisions.

Some organizations have transferred many of the traditional supervisory activities to their workers in the belief that giving the workers more authority to make decisions and take action results in:
- more efficient and effective work
- more effective and timely decision-making
- a decreased potential for mistakes because of reduced communication requirements (i.e. via a third party—the supervisor or team leader)

Management and operational systems are required to coordinate technology and tasks to achieve the mission.

To focus your efforts in the right places and manage your time effectively, you need to understand how your roles and responsibilities fit within your organization's management and operational systems. You also need to know what decisions you can and cannot make.

> As an example of how management style can affect employee decision-making, consider the following situation.
>
> An employee discovers a piece of equipment is not functioning properly. Depending on his or her roles and responsibilities, limits of authority, supervisor's expectations, and department policies, the employee's response could be one or more of the following actions:
> - fix the problem him- or herself
> - fill out a maintenance work order
> - discuss the issue with a peer
> - inform the team leader or supervisor
> - contact a vendor or contractor to service the equipment
> - note the issue in a log book
> - do nothing

Supervisors and work teams are responsible for achieving specific department and organizational results. Individual workers also have a responsibility to contribute to achieving specific department results.

Management sets the direction and establishes measurable goals. However, workers have a major influence on the results that are achieved. In practice, worker performance is a key factor in determining job performance which, in turn, determines corporate performance.

LEARNING ACTIVITY 5

Specify management and operational systems that impact the way you do your job

Management and operational systems have a major impact on the way you do your work and the results that you are to achieve. This learning activity helps you define the management and operational systems for your organization. Learning activities later in this section focus on the relationships of management and operational systems with other constituents of an organization.

5a.   There are many different ways to manage. From the three choices below, select the management style that is closest to defining your organization's management style.

☐ hierarchical (top down)

☐ like a baseball team (a coach that is part of the team)

☐ self-directed team (all members have the same authority and must reach a consensus when making decisions)

5b.   How effective is management in communicating to you the results that your department is to achieve this year?

☐ a lot

☐ somewhat

☐ a little

☐ very little

5c.   How effective is management at communicating to you how your work affects your department's results?

☐ a lot

☐ somewhat

☐ a little

☐ very little

5d.   How much authority do you have to make decisions that directly relate to your work including:

- how you do your work
- choosing tools and equipment to do the work
- collaborating with others
- dealing with problems
- communicating with external and internal customers

☐ a lot

☐ somewhat

☐ a little

☐ very little

2.5 Corporate Objectives

Each organization (large or small) has areas of concern such as safety, environment, equipment reliability, waste control, cost control, quality, and customer satisfaction. These areas of concern may be expressed through statements about vision, beliefs, practices, and policies. For each area of concern, the organization desires to either increase or decrease the effects on the organization, for example, decrease safety incidents, increase equipment reliability, decrease waste—these are the corporate objectives. Corporate objectives help workers identify what is important to the organization and where to focus their efforts.

The following table lists areas of concern, common to many organizations, for which corporate objectives may be developed.

Areas addressed by Corporate Objectives		
• safety	• energy use	• public image
• environment	• quality	• public disruption
• legislation	• waste control	• reputation
• equipment reliability and life	• loss control	• communication
• equipment optimization	• cost control	• teamwork
	• customer satisfaction	

Some organizations' business/corporate objectives and goals are written and continually monitored to determine the level of success in achieving them. Other organizations do not have written objectives and goals.

Whether or not your organization's objectives and goals are written, you need to understand the objectives that apply to your job. Understanding these objectives will help you focus your efforts effectively and make decisions in the best interest of your organization.

Section 5, *Strategic Business Objectives*, provides more information about corporate objectives and goals.

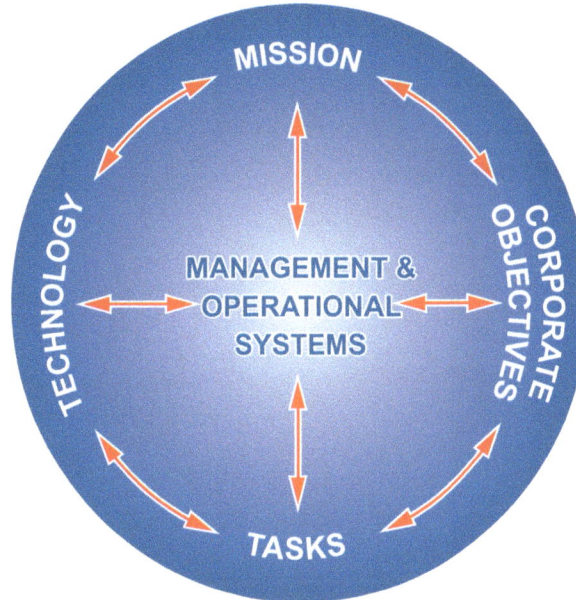

Corporate objectives provide direction for using technology, performing tasks, and coordinating work to effectively achieve the corporate mission.

LEARNING ACTIVITY 6

Specify your organization's corporate objectives

At the job level, corporate objectives are very useful. When you are performing tasks, the objectives help you focus your efforts on issues that are important to the organization. The corporate objectives also help you make effective decisions and provide leadership. This learning activity helps you identify and rank corporate objectives that are important to your job.

6a.   List a minimum of ten corporate objectives for your organization that give you guidance in carrying out your work and making decisions.

e.g., reduce safety incidents to zero _____

e.g., protect the environment _____

1.   _____

2.   _____

3. _____

4. _____

5. _____

6. _____

7. _____

8. _____

9. _____

10. _____

11. _____

12. _____

6b. Select a task you do that you think is critical to your organization. Rank the corporate objectives you have listed above from most important to least important in relation to the task. Note that the ranking of corporate objectives can change depending on the specific tasks being performed and the specific circumstances that arise. The higher ranked corporate objectives help determine where you must focus your efforts when doing that task.

Task _____

e.g., have zero safety incidents _____

e.g., protect the environment _____

1. _____

2. _____

3. _____

4. _____

5. _____

6. _____

7. _____

8. _____

9. _____

10. _____

11. _____

12. _____

Critical Thinking Questions

- What are the beliefs and values of my organization?

- What are my roles and responsibilities?

- Who are my internal and external customers?

- What are my limits of authority?

- What is the management style of this department?

- What are my department's goals for the year?

- How does my work contribute to achieving department goals?

- How does the quality of my work impact the organization?

- What corporate objectives are important to my department?

JobThink™

26

Relationship between Constituents

Each of the five constituents of an organization affects and is affected by each of the other constituents, as shown in the following illustration.

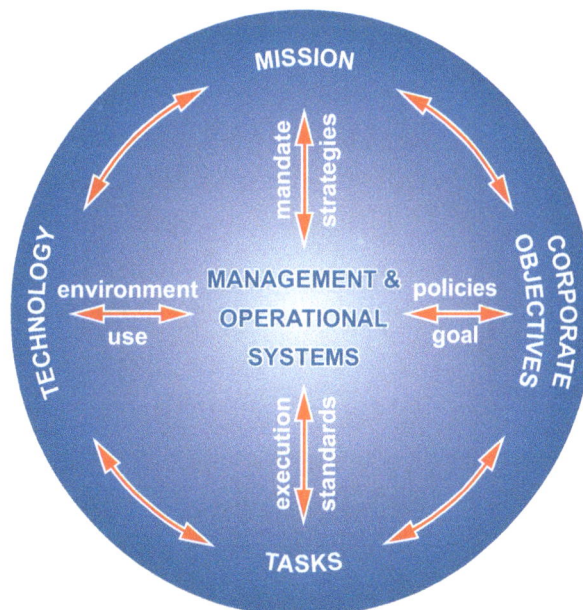

Relationship between constituents

3.1 Mission—Management and Operational Systems

Each department within an organization has a specific mandate, such as maintenance, operations, marketing, or accounting. The organization's beliefs, values, and strategies (i.e., mission) provide general direction to the department. Here are a few examples of directives:

- provide customized services
- manufacture high quality (and high priced) products
- target products to niche markets
- rapidly expand the business
- correct customer dissatisfaction at no cost to the customer
- operate equipment to failure
- provide just-in-time services
- minimize costs and expenditures
- establish working relationships between departments
- set priorities to meet short-term and/or long-term goals
- maintain ethical business practices

Departments use the beliefs, values, and business strategies as guiding principles for using resources (money, equipment, materials, people) and making decisions to achieve department and business goals. Sometimes business strategies lead to specific policies and practices. However, it is not practical to develop policies and practices for every possible situation. You need to understand your organization's business strategies so that you can be more effective in making decisions in situations that are not addressed by specific policies and practices.

LEARNING ACTIVITY 7

Identify your organization's business strategies, values, and beliefs

This learning activity helps you identify your organization's beliefs, values, and business strategies that provide the guiding principles for doing business and carrying out work.

7a. From your list in Leaning Activity 1a, give a specific example of a situation where your organization's business strategies, beliefs, or values *helped* you make a work-related decision.

_____

_____

_____

_____

_____

_____

7b.   From your list in Learning Activity 1a, give a specific example of a situation where you felt that the business strategy, belief, or value *inhibited* (or *prevented*) you from doing the best job you could do.

_____

_____

_____

_____

_____

_____

3.2 Mission—Corporate Objectives

Strategies provide the approaches and methods of carrying out business, whereas corporate objectives specify what is important to the organization and to business success. Corporate objectives often follow directly from belief statements, strategies, key success factors, and government legislation. Corporate objectives provide direction to departments and employees about what is important (e.g., ensuring safety of employees and the public, adhering to legislation, controlling quality, maximizing productivity). While you are working, corporate objectives help you direct your efforts and make decisions in the best interest of your organization.

3.3 Corporate Objectives—Management and Operational Systems

In support of the corporate objectives, departments (or the organization as a whole) establish policies, practices, and procedures that dictate how business is to be done and how work is to be carried out. Sometimes, specific policies and practices seem to make work more difficult. Often, corporate objectives provide the reasons that these policies or practices were established.

In some organizations, departments must establish numerical benchmarks (monthly or yearly) for each corporate objective. Actual department performance is monitored and compared with the benchmarks to determine the department's degree of success in achieving the corporate objectives.

LEARNING ACTIVITY 8

Identify your practices that are related to corporate objectives

Policies and practices often support corporate objectives or are driven by corporate objectives. Often corporate objectives provide the reasons for specific policies and practices. This learning activity helps you identify policies and practices that support corporate objectives or are created because of the corporate objectives.

8a. List three policies and/or practices that you believe were created to support your organization's corporate objectives.

1. _____

_____

2. _____

_____

3. _____

_____

8b.   Sometimes a policy or practice seems to make work more difficult and inefficient. State one such policy or practice and the corporate objective(s) that the policy or practice supports.

_____

_____

_____

_____

_____

_____

8c.   Do you feel that the policy or practice you identified in Learning Activity 8b is excessive or ineffective or is it appropriate for supporting the corporate objective(s)? Explain your choice.

_____

_____

_____

_____

_____

_____

_____

3.4 Mission—Technology

An organization decides on the type, quantity, and quality of technology (equipment, tools, and materials) used to achieve its mission. In industries, such as service and construction, technology is used to carry out tasks to achieve the mission. In the manufacturing and process industries, technology is the focus for achieving the mission.

From one organization to the next, the corporate strategy for selecting and maintaining equipment may vary, for example:

- using the newest and best equipment and tools versus *making do* with what you have
- ensuring equipment is standardized from one facility to the next versus using various types and models of equipment based on personal preference (e.g., of the engineers, maintenance personnel, and users), applications, and budget
- operating equipment with minimal maintenance until it fails versus applying a rigorous preventive maintenance program to extend equipment life and optimize the effectiveness and efficiency of equipment

Companies that have more than one facility may have a different strategy for each facility. For example, a company may have a large maintenance budget for a new facility that will be in operation for many years and a small maintenance budget for a facility that will be sold or closed in the near future.

For some industries, such as aeronautical, pipeline, and petrochemical, maintaining reliable equipment is important for protecting employees, the public, and the environment. For these industries, legislation dictates:

- the types and specifications of equipment and protective systems
- the maintenance required for specific equipment and the frequency of that maintenance

You need to understand your organization's business strategies related to the types, quality, and functionality of equipment, tools, and materials so that you can make effective decisions that support these strategies.

Your organization may also have a strategy related to equipment/material cost. More information about cost and cost control is provided in later sections of this book.

LEARNING ACTIVITY	9

Specify your organization's strategy regarding technology

The types, quality, and functionality of the equipment, tools and materials supplied by your organization affect your ability to do your job well.

9a. Using the right tools and equipment for the job is important for doing efficient, quality work and for working safely. For the jobs that you do, how appropriate are the *types* of tools and equipment supplied by your organization?

☐ very appropriate

☐ quite appropriate

☐ somewhat appropriate

☐ not very appropriate

9b. Well-made and reliable tools and equipment contribute to doing efficient, quality work. What is the quality of tools and equipment used in your job?

☐ very high quality

☐ quite high quality

☐ average quality

☐ poor quality

9c. Some tools and equipment function better than others. How well do the tools and equipment you use function?

☐ very well

☐ quite well

☐ somewhat well

☐ poorly

9d. What is your organization's strategy regarding maintaining the reliability and life of tools and equipment? Give an example to support your answer.

_____

_____

_____

_____

9e. Is your organization's strategy regarding maintaining the reliability and life of tools and equipment applied consistently? Provide an example to support your answer.

_____

_____

_____

_____

9f. For your organization's line of business, are equipment specifications and maintenance requirements legislated? If yes, provide an example.

_____

_____

_____

_____

3.5 Technology—Management and Operational Systems

Management is expected to optimize the use of technology, materials, and other resources—including people—to achieve corporate goals. Management is also expected to minimize loss and extend the life and use of equipment. Managers must justify budget requests and account for all funds allocated to their departments. Departments are given some direction for using the budgets to meet the productivity goals. Part of a budget may or may not be used to maintain, upgrade, or replace equipment and tools. Many factors, including business strategy and financial constraints, can affect the size and allocation of budgets.

Understanding the reasons behind your organization's strategies regarding quality, reliability, and the life of equipment, tools, and materials can be of value to you. This knowledge can help you determine what has priority and where to focus your efforts to preserve the quality and extend the life of technical and material resources. For example, some small tools and components are considered consumables and are discarded after one use because it can cost more to clean or repair them than to replace them. Most tools and equipment are critical to the business and must be kept in excellent condition to operate reliably. For example:

- Fixed safety systems, such as fire detection systems, must function reliably to provide early warning of unsafe conditions.
- Equipment, such as cranes, must function reliably to prevent injury.
- Protective devices on production equipment, such as high temperature shutdown switches, must operate reliably to shut the process down if the equipment fails.
- Mobile equipment, such as crawler tractors, must operate reliably to meet productivity goals.

LEARNING ACTIVITY 10

Specify the availability and reliability of tools and equipment

The availability and reliability of tools and equipment affect your ability to do your job well. Knowing your organization's strategy regarding the availability and reliability of tools and equipment helps you to:

- make better decisions regarding the use and care of equipment
- be more tolerant (and patient) when budgets restrict the purchase and maintenance of tools and equipment

This learning activity focuses on your organization's position regarding the availability and reliability of tools and equipment.

10a. How important is it to your organization to ensure the availability of tools and equipment?

☐ very high importance

☐ quite high importance

☐ some importance

☐ low importance

10b. How important is it to your organization to ensure the reliability of tools and equipment?

☐ very high importance

☐ quite high importance

☐ some importance

☐ low importance

10c. List three tools, equipment, and/or systems that must be reliable to meet your organization's goals.

_____

_____

_____

10d. State the consequences if the tools, equipment, and/or systems are not available or function poorly.

_____

_____

_____

10e. Give reasons for your organization's position regarding the availability and reliability of tools and equipment.

_____

_____

_____

3.6 Tasks—Technology

In industries, such as manufacturing and process, the technology is the focus for achieving the mission. In these industries, many tasks, but not all, stem from the need to install, operate, and maintain the technology. Operating and maintenance procedures and standards are developed for the specific equipment.

In industries, such as service and construction, carrying out tasks is the focus for achieving the mission. Technology is used to assist in carrying out the tasks. Standards and procedures focus on using the technology safely and effectively to achieve the desired results.

Generally, you are expected to use and care for tools, equipment, and materials in ways that maintain their quality and functionality and extend their life. It is also expected that, when this technology is damaged or functions poorly, you report the problem so that corrective action can be taken.

The book *EquipThink* provides strategies for using tools and equipment effectively and extending equipment life.

| LEARNING ACTIVITY 11 | Specify the protocols for reporting damaged tools and equipment |

Protocol:

procedure, rule, code of behavior, expected way of doing something

You are expected to take care of your organization's equipment, tools, and materials. In Learning Activity 4, you stated the relationship between tasks and technology for your job. This relationship can affect how and to whom you report damaged tools and equipment. This learning activity focuses on the reporting processes you must follow when you identify damaged equipment, tools, or materials.

11a. Through their actions, people can reduce the life of tools, equipment, and systems. Provide three examples where people's actions have reduced the life of tools, equipment and/or systems.

_____

_____

_____

_____

_____

11b. What are you supposed to do if you discover damaged tools and equipment?

_____

_____

_____

_____

11c. To whom do you verbally report damaged tools and equipment?

_____

_____

_____

11d. What written documentation is required when reporting damaged tools and equipment? To whom do you submit the written documentation?

_____

_____

_____

_____

_____

3.7 Tasks—Management and Operational Systems

Management has a number of responsibilities that affect the workplace, including:

- setting up work groups (e.g., job positions and job families) and determining the staffing requirements for each group
- establishing the lines and limits of authority for each job position and in some cases for each employee within a job position
- establishing the selection process and placement qualifications for job positions
- delegating work and coordinating employees within a job position and between job positions
- identifying gaps in employee performance and identifying training methods. In some government jurisdictions, legislation dictates that the organization must prove that employees are competent to perform specific tasks. For example, in the United States, the Office of Pipeline Safety's Operator Qualification program requires companies to demonstrate that operators and maintenance personnel are competent to perform critical tasks. Critical tasks are those that could affect public safety and the environment should the tasks be performed poorly.

In unionized work environments, job descriptions and what a worker can and cannot do may be specified. Workers in self-directed work groups may be able to negotiate the tasks they want to do. Organizations also differ in their degree of commitment and flexibility for workers to learn new skills as part of their personal career development.

Supervisors and team leaders (management) are responsible for establishing work processes and standards which reflect corporate strategies and objectives. Influences outside a department can also have an effect on standards. For example:

- other company departments (e.g., safety, health, environment, engineering, and accounting)
- government legislation
- customers
- specialized employees, such as information technologists

NOTE

The methods used to establish policies, practices, and procedures depend on management style (e g , dictated by management or developed by the participation of workers and specialists). Some organizations may be flexible in establishing policies, practices, and procedures. For example, they may dictate policies in response to changes in legislation but may prefer to have workers and specialists involved when work-related issues need addressing.

The book *WorkThink* provides instructions on work processes and performance standards for working safely, effectively, efficiently, and with the least amount of effort to achieve the desired results (i.e., how and how well tasks are performed).

For many work projects, management coordinates the work performed by different work groups. Within each work group, each worker is responsible for planning and working in ways that harmonize with the work being done by others. To effectively contribute to job and corporate performance, you must be able to coordinate your work with that of other workers and work groups. Section 6 of this book addresses coordination of work.

LEARNING ACTIVITY 12

Specify how management and operational systems affect job assignments, how and how well tasks are performed, and product quality

This learning activity focuses on how your organization establishes work groups and delegates work. The learning activity also addresses how your organization makes changes to job assignments, methods of work, and quality of work.

12a. My discipline is_____

_____

Other work groups or departments that affect my work:

_____

_____

_____

_____

12b. Briefly describe the process your organization uses to establish or change policies and practices.

_____

_____

_____

_____

_____

_____

12c. Sometimes changes to work processes may be made to address specific issues. These changes could involve creating new tasks. For example, in a custom fabrication shop, there is a need to ensure that materials for customer orders are available to prevent downtime and delays. The decision by management has been made to have a second person double check inventory to ensure that materials are available to fill orders for the next three days. Management could assign the task to someone, ask for volunteers, or have the work group make the decision as to who should do the inventory check.

Describe the process used to assign new tasks in your work group.

_____

_____

_____

_____

12d. In some organizations, the way work is done may be well established and does not change (e.g., work station of a manufacturing production line). In other organizations, the worker has the freedom to decide how to do the work. To what degree do you have the freedom to decide how you will go about performing tasks? Give an example of a task to support your answer.

_____

_____

_____

_____

12e. Co-workers, other work groups, departments, and customers can affect when a task will be performed. In your job position, provide an example of when the timing of a task can be affected by other work groups or customers.

_____

_____

_____

12f. Organizations establish standards for performing tasks and for product quality. These standards may also be set by industry or the customer.

How have the standards for work performance and product quality been established for your job position?

_____

_____

What would cause these standards to change?

_____

_____

_____

What process would be used to change the standards?

_____

_____

_____

12g. In addition to providing legislated safety training, organizations can provide job-specific or site-specific training.

What job-specific training or site-specific training does your organization provide so that you can do your tasks to the expected standards?

_____

_____

_____

How is the training delivered?

_____

_____

While being trained, how do you know you are doing the task(s) satisfactorily?

_____

_____

_____

3.8 Tasks—Corporate Objectives

Your organization's corporate objectives can guide you in making day-to-day work decisions. For example, corporate objectives can help you:
- determine the order of priority of doing work when there are several tasks that need to be done
- determine where to focus your efforts (i.e., decide what is important) when doing a task. For example, safety, equipment condition, and product quality may be more important than getting the work done quickly and with the least amount of cost.

- make decisions in the best interest of the organization. For example, in response to a change in conditions or an event, you can use corporate objectives to identify the consequences that will impact your organization.
- determine the best response to an undesired event. For example, in response to a hazardous material spill, you may decide, based on your organization's priorities, that protecting the environment is more important than meeting customer schedules. You would then take action accordingly.

When you make job-related decisions, you must:
- determine the consequences of a condition or action
- determine what is important to the organization for decision-making (i.e., order the corporate objectives by priority)
- determine the standards that must be met (originating from technology, management, corporate objectives, and customers)
- consider the limits of your authority to take action (originating from management)
- adhere to corporate policies and practices when taking action (originating from management, corporate objectives, mission, and government legislation)

Decision-making is explained in more detail in Section 8 of this book.

LEARNING ACTIVITY 13

Use corporate objectives to determine what is important when performing tasks

Corporate objectives are very useful to you for deciding on the order in which tasks should be done and in determining where to focus your effort when doing tasks (i.e., what is important). This learning activity gives you the opportunity to apply corporate objectives to the tasks you perform.

13. Select a work-related problem that does not affect safety or the environment.

    Problem: _____

    _____

The ranking of importance of corporate objectives can change for different tasks and problems. Using the list of corporate objectives from Learning Activity 6a, rank the objectives to best describe their order of importance regarding the problem you identified above. For example, the effect of the problem on equipment availability may be of greatest concern and its effect on customers may be the next most important concern.

_____

_____

_____

_____

_____

_____

_____

_____

_____

_____

NOTE

The previous descriptions of the relationship between constituents only deal with the constituents that are directly related to each other. The relationships between mission and tasks and between technology and corporate objectives are not described in this book. For example, technology can be used to improve safety (a corporate objective) and mission, through the management and operational systems, affects how work is performed and the standards for doing tasks.

Marketing and finance have been indirectly built into this business model. For example, financing affects the resources used to do the work and the degree of commitment to ensuring customer satisfaction. However, these constituents or others could be added to form a three-dimensional model. If you are part of a department that provides management and administrative support such as engineering or accounting, you may find it useful to identify you department's service as a separate constituent. By doing so, you may find it easier to determine relationships with other constituents such as mission and corporate objectives.

Relating sets of constituents to one another is a practical way of presenting issues that affect workers and their abilities to be effective. When you are confronted with a new task or work condition, you can use the model to determine what to do and where to put your efforts to effectively contribute to job and corporate performance.

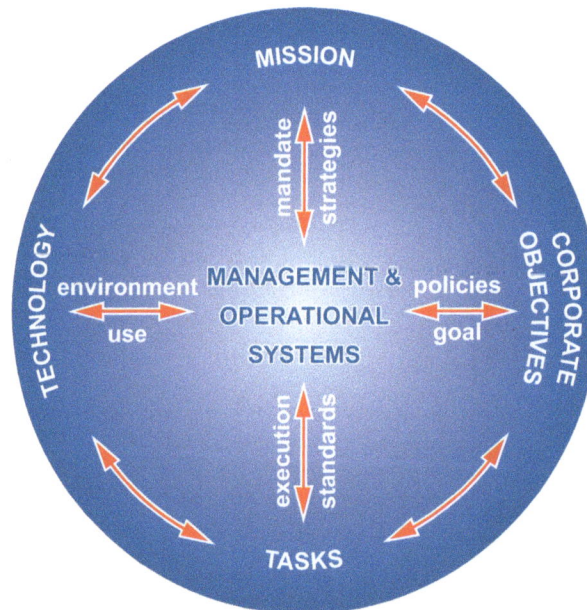

Relationship of constituents.

Critical Thinking Questions
• What quality of equipment does this organization use?
• What is my organization's strategy for maintaining equipment?
• What equipment must operate reliably?
• How can I contribute to the reliability of equipment?
• How can I extend the life of equipment?
• How do I report damaged equipment?
• What are the most important tasks?
• What are the most important aspects of this task?

Section 4

Resources

Most organizations need four resources to function:
- money
- equipment
- materials
- people

Depending on the organization's line of business, the need for these resources varies. For example, service organizations may need minimal equipment and a large workforce, whereas manufacturers may need a large investment in equipment and a small workforce. In all organizations, resources must be used effectively to maximize productivity.

This section:
- provides a basic description of why organizations must make effective use of these four resources and how these resources may affect your work
- describes your roles and responsibilities for using these our resources effectively to contribute to your organization's success

4.1 Money

Money is an essential resource for all organizations. Money is needed to buy equipment and materials and meet operating expenses. Unless the company is publicly traded, workers often do not have an accurate understanding of the organization's financial wellbeing. Workers tend to underestimate the costs of doing business and overestimate profit. In poor economic times, workers may not have an accurate understanding of the organization's financial difficulties.

Workers often have an understanding about the costs for equipment, materials, and labor but underestimate overheads such as employee benefits, insurance, office leases, legal and accounting services, marketing costs, administrative services, and interest on debt.

Cash Flow

For businesses, making a profit is essential for survival. The shareholders of publicly-traded companies expect a reasonable return on their investment. If the value of the company's shares decreases, the value of the business decreases. The business then has difficulty arranging financing to make capital purchases and meet operating costs, including salaries. Cash flow can become an issue. Because there are often delays of one to three months before being paid for services and products, companies must have considerable cash resources to cover operating costs for several months.

Example of Cash Flow Demands

- work one month and immediately send invoices for work done ($100,000). This $100,000 is now called a receivable. It takes 3 months before the receivable is paid.
- 95% expenses
- 5% profit
- pay all expenses at the end of each month
- $95,000 expenses
- $5,000 profit
- $100,000 receivables per month
- Cash flow requirements to cover three invoice periods while waiting to receive the first $100,000 = $285,000.00 ($95,000 X 3)
- profit $15,000.00 ($5,000 X 3). First $5,000 profit received at end of the third month.

(continued)

> **Spending Profits**
>
> After receiving the first $100,000, management can use the $5,000 profit in various ways to meet business goals, for example:
> - pay down debt
> - keep cash for contingency should problems develop
> - purchase new equipment
> - hire more employees
> - increase salaries
> - provide training
> - increase marketing activities
>
> In a competitive market and in times of reduced revenues, organizations must continually identify ways of reducing costs and increasing efficiencies. More attention may also have to be given to ensure cash flow requirements are met.

Budgets

As part of financial management, departments are given specific budgets and directions on how to use the budget. Budgets can have a major impact at the job level, affecting:
- the quality and availability of tools and equipment
- the quality of materials
- the quality of the work environment
- the number of workers and their individual workloads
- the type and amount of workplace training
- wages and benefits

The need to use budgets wisely is often the basis for policies and practices to control costs, minimize losses, and use resources efficiently. In some cases, restrictive budgets are counterproductive to meeting business objectives. For example, worn-out equipment may cause excessive downtime and increase maintenance costs; using low-grade materials can make work more difficult and inefficient. Sometimes, cost-saving measures can cause customer dissatisfaction, a situation that may harm the organization over the long term.

Longer-term goals can also affect budgets. For example, if a company plans to expand or buy out a competitor, the need for additional financing may result in restricted operating and maintenance budgets.

Poor tracking and billing of expenses can also affect budgets. Workers must accurately document timesheets and expenses so that these costs are included in invoicing. Accurate documentation of expenses is also important for setting product prices and service rates.

LEARNING ACTIVITY 14

Identify how budgets can have a major impact at the job level

This learning activity addresses how financial considerations can have immediate as well as long-term impacts at the job level (and on you).

14a. For your job position, list three cost-related issues where you must pay special attention to control costs.

1. _____
2. _____
3. _____

14b. The economy is slow and your organization's revenues are decreasing. Identify the three most likely ways your organization would reduce costs.

1. _____
2. _____
3. _____

14c. The economy is healthy and your organization decides to expand. For your area of work, identify three items for which your organization's budget would likely increase.

1. _____
2. _____
3. _____

4.2 Equipment

This section describes types and quality of equipment and your responsibilities when working around and using equipment.

For this book, the term *equipment* is used to include:
- hand and power tools
- mobile and stationary equipment (including vehicles)

Type and Quality of Equipment

The type of equipment used to perform tasks affects the methods and the procedures for carrying out the work. For example, a hand saw, portable electric saw, table saw, radial arm saw, and chain saw may all be available for completing a task. The specific task application and the desired quality of results may determine which saw to use. Use of some equipment may be restricted. For example, a table saw may be set up and used only to cut plywood and plastic laminate. You may not have authorization to use a specific piece of equipment until you have received training.

The quality of the equipment varies among organizations in the same line of business. Business strategies, financial ability, market factors, competition, and corporate goals may affect decisions to invest in equipment. The quality and condition of the equipment that is available to some degree affects your ability to do a task safely, effectively, efficiently, and with minimal effort. Generally, lower-priced equipment tends not to function as well as higher-priced equipment. Conversely, expensive equipment may not function better than moderately-priced equipment. Other factors such as life expectancy, warranty, turnaround time for repair, and safety features must also be taken into account when selecting and purchasing equipment.

Government regulations may also dictate the type, design, condition, and use of equipment, for example:
- use of safety guards on rotating parts
- use of personal protective equipment when operating equipment
- ventilation and lighting requirements
- requirement that the equipment be in good operating condition

• requirement to lock out equipment that is being unjammed, checked, or repaired

Your Responsibilities for Equipment

When working around and using equipment, you are responsible for:

• ensuring the safe, efficient, and effective use of equipment
• contributing to equipment reliability
• extending equipment life
• minimizing energy consumption
• reporting/repairing damaged or malfunctioning equipment
• working within your organization's lines and limits of authority

If you are dissatisfied with the quantity, quality, or type of tools and equipment that are available, knowing the reasons the organization does not make improvements can help you be more understanding. Conversely, if you identify how changes to the tools and equipment can significantly improve work effectiveness and efficiency, you should inform decision-makers of the opportunities for improving productivity.

The book *EquipThink* addresses the selection and operation of tools and equipment.

LEARNING ACTIVITY 15

Describe equipment quality, care, and reliability

Learning Activity 15 involves the quality and reliability of equipment. This learning activity primarily focuses on how the quality of equipment impacts your ability to perform your work effectively and efficiently.

15a. If the quality and availability of equipment were to improve, to what degree could you perform your work more effectively and efficiently?

☐ a lot

☐ quite a bit

☐ some

☐ a little

15b. What factors affect the selection of equipment for your job position (e.g., initial cost, safety features, functionality, warranty)?

_____

_____

_____

_____

15c. How does the way you work affect equipment condition? Provide an example.

_____

_____

_____

_____

15d. How does the way you work affect equipment life? Provide an example.

_____

_____

_____

_____

15e. In your line of work, list a piece of equipment for which a worker must have training before he or she can use the equipment.

_____

_____

4.3 Materials

Materials come in many different forms and have many different uses:
- raw materials (unprocessed ore, plastic pellets)
- semi-finished materials (plywood, rolled steel)

- finished materials (plastic laminate, plate glass)
- consumables (solvents, paint rollers)

Previous sections of this book addressed some of the issues you need to consider when processing raw materials and manufacturing semi-finished and finished materials. This section focuses on making effective use of semi-finished materials, finished materials, and consumables.

Type and Quality of Materials

Organizations want to keep the use of materials to a practical minimum to control costs. At the same time, consideration must be given to the type and quality of materials because they can impact productivity and customer safety and satisfaction.

While some materials may cost less than others, their characteristics (e.g., strength, finish, machinability) may make them difficult to use (and they may not meet the customer's expectations). If you have choices in selecting materials, one important consideration for maximizing productivity is to take into account the tradeoff between the costs of different materials and the efficiency of working with them.

Sometimes manufacturers and suppliers change the quality or characteristics of the materials you use. You may or may not be informed of the changes. Sometimes, you only discover the change in quality long after the materials are in use. At other times, you may discover the change in materials immediately because they machine differently than previous batches. You may need to use different tools and pay special attention to how you work to minimize damage and maintain productivity. You may also need to make sure the new materials meet your customer's requirements.

Minimize Waste

Minimizing waste is an important strategy for controlling costs and protecting the environment. Part of your pre-work planning is to consider ways to use materials so that waste is kept to a practical minimum.

Minimize waste

- *use the right material for the job*
- *measure twice, cut once*

To minimize the overall costs of materials, you should consider strategies such as:

- reducing the use of materials
- reusing materials and consumables
- recycling materials
- exchanging materials with other companies

Of concern is to ensure the cost associated with reusing, recycling, and exchanging materials is less than the cost for purchasing new materials. Some organizations are willing to pay an extra cost as part of their commitment to protecting the environment.

Protecting the environment and controlling costs also involve the use of energy. Reducing the use of energy and limiting the amount of emissions from fuel combustion contribute to protecting the environment.

Environmental issues important to workers are addressed in detail in the book *EnviroThink*.

LEARNING ACTIVITY 16

Use materials wisely

For some organizations, the cost-effective use of materials is a very important consideration affecting the viability of the business. This learning activity focuses on how to make cost-effective use of materials.

16a. Provide one or more examples of materials for which your organization is cost-sensitive.

_____

_____

_____

16b. For your job position, provide an example of a strategy to maximize the use of a material.

_____

_____

16c. Give an example where a higher quality material would make your work more efficient and/or improve the quality of your work.

_____

_____

_____

16d. For your job position, provide an example where a higher quality material would **not** improve productivity (e.g. replacing twist winch cable with non-twist winch cable).

_____

_____

16e. For your job position, provide an example of a material that is/could be reused, recycled, or exchanged to reduce the impact on the environment.

_____

_____

4.4 People

This section describes an organization's written directives for meeting business objectives. The section also describes your responsibilities for performing work satisfactorily.

People at all levels of an organization play important roles to ensure that the organization is effective and successful. Senior members (e.g., directors, presidents, and chief executive officers) are expected to provide leadership and make decisions in the best interest of the organization. Their vision and goals for the organization must fit the marketplace and meet customer expectations and demands.

To achieve the vision and goals for the organization, strategies for success must be executed effectively. Senior staff set expectations but the effectiveness of people at the operational level often determines business results.

Strategic Business Objectives

Senior staff must effectively communicate their expectations to operational people so that everyone in the organization focuses their efforts in the desired direction... to coin a phrase, *so that everyone is riding on the same bus and heading in the same direction.* One way to communicate expectations is through written Strategic Business Objectives (SBOs). SBOs are those objectives that the organization believes critical for business success. Refer to Section 5, *Strategic Business Objectives* for more information.

Work Directives: Policies, Guidelines, Practices, Procedures

At the operational level, strategic business objectives provide direction but may not effectively address how the objectives are to be achieved. Policies, guidelines, and practices provide general direction about how the work and jobs are to be done. However, within the stated limits, operations staff may be allowed to adjust the methods of work and use of resources in response to different work conditions and job requirements.

> **Policy**—Rule, guideline, practice
>
> **Guideline**—provides suggestions about the resources and methods to be used to perform a specific work assignment or to respond to a specific condition or event. The purpose of a guideline is to provide general direction to the employee. Within the guideline, the employee has the latitude and flexibility to make changes in response to different work conditions.
>
> **Practice**—specifies the way an organization does business. A practice can specify the requirements, such as resources, employee qualifications, and general methodology, that must be used or in place when carrying out specific work or responding to specific conditions or events.
>
> **Procedure**—step-by-step actions to safely, effectively, and efficiently carry out a task to a specific standard. A procedure may also specify tools, equipment, components, safety requirements, and employee qualifications required to do the work.

Some tasks are considered critical because of their impact on the organization:

- they must be performed well to contribute to the business goals
- if they are performed poorly, the organization could experience losses (e.g., injuries, damage to the environment, waste, returned product, loss of customers)

For critical tasks, procedures and standards provide very specific directions on how and how well the tasks are to be performed.

The book *WorkThink* provides detailed information on standards for tasks and ways to perform tasks safely, effectively, and efficiently with the least amount of effort.

Written directives (i.e., SBOs, policies, guidelines, practices, procedures, and standards) provide direction and the expectations for performing work. To ensure the directives are executed effectively, management must use a systematic approach which:

- reinforces the importance of following the directives
- ensures that operations staff can access the written directives
- ensures that operations staff have the resources and competence (knowledge and skills) to carry out the directives

Your Responsibilities

Within your roles and responsibilities, you need to understand the strategic business objectives and written directives so that you can focus your efforts in the same direction as everyone else in the organization. You also have a responsibility to ensure that you are competent to perform the work satisfactorily. You may also have a responsibility to help train others to become competent.

Many organizations recognize the importance of having competent workers to achieve business success. At the same time, governments and customers are becoming more demanding that workers be competent. To ensure workers can perform work competently, organizations use a variety of methods, such as:

- hiring people who have the training and experience to do the work

- requiring operations staff to demonstrate that they are competent to perform specific tasks
- providing on-the-job coaching and mentorship
- providing competency-based training
- closely supervising and monitoring staff performance
- gathering feedback about staff performance from internal and external customers
- providing feedback to staff about their performance. When gaps in performance are identified, provide assistance to fill the performance gaps (e.g., clarify performance expectations, provide refresher training).
- providing encouragement and incentives (e.g., new work assignments, promotions, job security) to do well
- providing opportunities for staff to learn new or different types of work

Many types of work change over time. New materials, equipment, changing customer expectations, and new legislation can change the way you work. You have a responsibility to your organization and to yourself to keep your knowledge and skills current and to continually strive to maintain and expand your capabilities. Being recognized for excellent performance can contribute to your job satisfaction. Continually learning new skills can lead to opportunities within your organization to take on new or different challenges. Continually improving your abilities also puts you in a strong competitive position for employment outside of your organization.

LEARNING ACTIVITY 17

Work effectively

People are a very important resource for an organization. This learning activity focuses on the importance of working in ways that contribute to business success.

17a. Select a guideline for doing work in your area. Explain what changes in work conditions would make it important for you to be able to change the way you do the work.

_____

_____

_____

_____

_____

17b. State a practice for doing work in your area and explain why the practice is important to your organization.

_____

_____

_____

_____

_____

17c. Identify a critical procedure and explain why the procedure is critical to achieving business goals or preventing losses.

_____

_____

_____

_____

17d. Describe job-specific or site-specific training your organization provides and give reasons why the training must be specific to your job/site.

_____

_____

_____

_____

17e. Explain how your organization provides feedback about your performance.

_____

_____

_____

17f. Give examples of how your organization provides encouragement and incentives to do well.

_____

_____

_____

17g. Give examples of how your organization provides opportunities for learning new job skills.

_____

_____

_____

Critical Thinking Questions

- What are the critical cost-related issues of my job?
- What equipment do I need to do this job safely, effectively, and efficiently?
- How can I make the best use of materials?
- What am I supposed to do with waste?
- How can I protect the environment?
- How are decisions made regarding change?
- What tasks are considered critical?
- Can I decide on my own how to do the work?
- What policies and practices are important to doing my work?
- How do I know I am doing the tasks satisfactorily?
- How can I work more safely, effectively, and efficiently?
- What job-specific training does the organization provide?

Section 5

Strategic Business Objectives

Strategic business objectives (SBOs) focus on aspects of the business in which the organization believes it must perform with excellence to be successful. SBOs are general statements that reflect corporate values and are derived from the organization's mission and business concepts. Examples of the general focus of SBOs include:

- shareholder expectations
- customer satisfaction
- competitiveness
- safety and environment
- public stakeholders
- culture

An organization uses one or more strategies to achieve a specific SBO. For example, customer satisfaction may be achieved by strategies such as:

- providing reliable products
- providing timely service
- guaranteeing the lowest price
- applying a long-term marketing cycle

Strategies for reducing costs may include:

- improving technology
- reducing waste

- using just-in-time inventory controls
- reducing staffing
- implementing maintenance management software
- improving employee performance and job satisfaction

SBOs and strategies may or may not be documented. In either case, you are expected to understand what is important to your organization and to support the SBOs and strategies. Your organization's written policies, guidelines, practices, and procedures help you do your work in ways that contribute to job and corporate performance. Some of these documented directives have been created to help achieve specific SBOs. If you understand the reasons for the directives, you may be more prepared to accept the directives as beneficial rather than unnecessary.

Critical Success Indicators and Benchmarks

Some organizations continually monitor their strategic business objectives to determine the level of success in achieving the objectives. *Critical success indicators* and *benchmarks* may be used to measure and assess success. Critical success indicators include incident index, equipment runtime, percentage of rejected product, total throughput, quantity of waste, cost per unit, total sales, market share, and customer satisfaction index.

The critical success indicators are documented monthly and compared with the benchmarks to determine the department's/ organization's success in achieving the goals. This information is shared with everyone in the organization to celebrate successes and to determine how to improve in areas of deficiency. Once a year, upper management may review the SBOs, benchmarks, and actual department performance. Benchmarks may be adjusted and an action plan developed to improve areas of deficiency.

Your Responsibilities

The department and each worker have a responsibility to work towards achieving the benchmarks. You can use the information that is shared about your department's performance to better focus your efforts to contribute to job and corporate performance. For those benchmarks that are being achieved, you most likely are doing the right things and doing them right. For those benchmarks where there are performance gaps, you need to determine how you can adjust your ways of working to better contribute to reducing the performance gaps.

Sometimes, organizations implement new programs and systems to be more effective at achieving the SBOs, for example:
- loss control programs
- reliability maintenance programs
- quality assurance programs
- environment management programs
- administration systems software programs

<table>
<tr><td>LEARNING
ACTIVITY</td><td>18</td></tr>
</table>

Contribute to business success

This learning activity focuses on ways you can work to contribute to achieving business success.

18a. SBOs for your organization may or may not be formally written statements. List three SBOs for your organization.

1. _____

2. _____

3. _____

18b. For your area of work, list three strategies used to contribute to achieving the SBOs.

1. _____

2. _____

3. _____

18c. Does your organization use benchmarks as part of monitoring organizational performance?

☐ Yes   ☐ No

If yes, provide three examples of benchmarks.

1. _____

2. _____

3. _____

18d. Provide an example of how you might be able to work differently to contribute to improving your organization's performance.

_____

_____

_____

Critical Thinking Questions

- What are my organization's strategic business objectives?
- What are the benchmarks for the SBOs?
- What strategies does the organization use to achieve the SBOs?
- How can I contribute to achieving the SBOs?

Impact of Work on Other Workers

In theory, individual workers, groups of workers, and departments should work together cooperatively *like the components of a well-oiled machine.* In practice, however, cooperation can break down, leading to inefficiencies and decreased quality. Some of the reasons cooperation breaks down include conflicts of interest between individuals, work groups, and departments; a lack of planning; ineffective communication; and self-serving values.

Poor timing, poor sequencing of activities, lack of quality, bottlenecks: these are all signs of poor collaboration. Often these work problems stem from a failure to understand the impacts that individuals, groups, and departments have on each other. You need to understand how your work affects others and how other individuals, groups, and departments affect your work. This knowledge can help you anticipate how your work may adversely affect others and, when possible, make adjustments.

Following is an example showing where a lack of quality at one stage of a production line affects another stage of production.

Stage 3 makes steel bases and pre-drills holes for bolting on equipment. Stage 4 bolts the equipment onto the pre-drilled steel bases. The holes in the bases do not align with the holes in the equipment. The result of the misaligned holes can create losses to people, equipment, materials, the environment, and the organization (PEMEO*):

People lost time, frustration, loss of respect for the workers responsible for the low-quality work

Equipment stress on mounted equipment

Materials some bases must be scrapped, increased cost of materials, increased landfill costs

Environment some parts of the rejected bases cannot be recycled and are disposed of in a land fill

Organization customer orders not filled on time, customer dissatisfaction, loss of profit

* Each of the five categories of PEMEO is called a *domain*. The term *domain* is used in Section 8—*Solving Problems* to specify who or what is affected by a problem.

This section describes:
- the coordination of work between:
  - individual workers
  - groups of specialists
  - departments
- the coordination of shared tools and equipment
- the impact of technical and work process changes
- how to work with others to contribute to job and corporate performance

6.1 Coordinating Work between Individual Workers

Sometimes, two or more workers together complete basic tasks such as handling large, awkwardly shaped, or heavy materials. If the activity is not timed well, workers can be injured and materials damaged. For example, a worker can receive serious cuts if two workers handling large sheets of light gauge metal do not time their actions. Communication about what has to be done, how it is to be done, and the timing of actions can reduce injuries and damage. Communicating about the next action a worker will be taking may be required.

Sometimes two workers must coordinate their specific tasks to achieve a common goal, for example, the coordination between a signaler and a crane operator. The signaler trusts that the crane operator follows the signals accurately and takes into account the work conditions (e.g., adjusts rate of travel). The crane operator trusts that the signaler is timing the signals so that he or she (the crane operator) can respond safely and effectively. In this case, coordination relies on effective communication and timing.

A worker may have to coordinate his or her activities to meet the needs of another worker. For example, a dentist may be working with three different patients at the same time. The dentist's assistant must anticipate the dentist's actions and do the right things, in the right order, and at the right times so that all patients receive efficient and effective service.

6.2 Coordinating Work between Groups of Specialists

Often, several workers share tasks to complete a job. For example, when laying sod, the timing of work activities is important: one or more workers grades, another worker moves the pallets of sod close to the work area, and other workers lay the sod. Grading should start several hours before the sod is laid so that the sod layers do not have to wait for the grading to be completed. Sod must be available when the sod layers are ready to start work. The pallet mover must place the sod in locations convenient for the sod layers without damaging the graded landscape or interfering with the work. A bottleneck could occur if the graders can't keep ahead of the sod layers; for example, if the graders didn't start early enough, if the graders don't have enough workers, if powered equipment fails, or if soil conditions are difficult for laying sod. In this case, the timing of activities is an important factor to ensure the work is completed efficiently.

In some projects, the work of specialist groups must be sequenced and coordinated so that the project is completed efficiently and effectively. In building construction, for example, specialists such as plumbers, electricians, and heating, ventilation, and air conditioning workers can work at the same time, as long as:

- different specialists do not work in the same area at the same time so that they don't interfere with each other or create a risk of a safety incident
- the components installed by one group of specialists do not interfere with the installation of components by other specialists
- materials for one group of specialists are not placed in areas that impede the work being done by other specialists

NOTE

For some service companies, delays due to late service of specialists can lead to large penalties if other specialists must be on standby waiting to start work.

One common problem in businesses that have twenty-four hour operations is handing over shifts. Two issues are often cited:

- one shift crew uses different work methods that cause concern or, at a minimum, irritation for the next crew
- communication between successive shift crews is incomplete and ineffective

6.3 Coordinating Work between Departments

Often, departments such as operations, maintenance, and warehousing must coordinate their work. For example, the repair of equipment in a process or production line may require that:

- maintenance personnel time repair work to minimize the impact on production and customers
- operations personnel shut down and make the equipment safe before maintenance begins work
- warehouse personnel have the right type and quantity of replacement components available by the time maintenance work starts
- operations personnel are available to temporarily start and stop the equipment upon request of maintenance personnel
- after the equipment is repaired, maintenance and operations personnel coordinate their pre-start checks to ensure the equipment is safe to start up
- if the equipment is part of a process or production line, operations personnel coordinate the starting of the equipment with other operational activities

6.4 Coordinating the Use of Shared Tools and Equipment

Individuals and work groups may have to share specialty tools and equipment. In this situation, the timing of work activities is critical for ensuring that the tools and equipment are available when needed. Pre-planning and effective ongoing communication between individual workers and work groups are required to ensure effective resource sharing.

In large organizations that have facilities at more than one location, there is a good possibility that at one or more locations there are shortages or overstocking of warehouse items, such as components, tools, and equipment. Some warehouse items may need to be special ordered and take months to arrive. If one location is short of a special order item and needs it immediately to maintain productivity, another location may be able to supply it. Competitors will sometimes lend components and tools to each other if the problem is urgent.

6.5 Impact of Technical and Work Process Changes

In processes where there are several systems, changes in operating variables, such as temperature, pressure, and production rates of one system can have adverse effects on other systems. The changes can downgrade the efficiencies and quality of the other systems and potentially put workers at risk of injury.

In work processes, one work group may change work methods to make the work easier, more efficient, or more cost-effective. However, the changes could create problems for other work groups:

- a change in quality or product specifications could:
  - affect the efficiency and effectiveness of downstream work groups
  - create a safety hazard for other work groups
- changes in the timing of services and delivery of products could affect the efficiency and effectiveness of other groups
- upstream groups could experience a bottleneck

WARNING

Sometimes workers think of ways to make the work easier, more effective and efficient, or safer. However, a change made to optimize a task may harm other people and work processes; care must be taken to ensure that the change does not have a negative impact on equipment, technical systems, and work processes. Optimizing a technical process without considering the total operation can lead to unpredicted changes in equipment and process variables such as pressure and temperature. Equipment may be subjected to excessive stress or extreme environments that degrade the equipment over time or cause immediate failure. Vendors, engineers, and loss control specialists may have to be consulted before any changes are made to ensure the proposed changes will not cause losses.

Some organizations have a formal management of change (MOC) process. Before any changes are made, a rigorous assessment of the impacts of change on PEMEO (People, Equipment, Materials, Environment, Organization) is carried out to ensure the changes will not downgrade the operation.

6.6 Working with Others to Contribute to Job and Corporate Performance

Often workers and work groups do not fully understand the issues and concerns of other work groups and departments. Consequently, the workers and work groups may not understand how their work impacts others. Within your roles and responsibilities, you need to understand:

- how your work impacts other workers and departments
- how other workers and departments can affect your productivity

Ask other workers about how your work affects them. Some areas of concern for which you can ask questions are:

- how your work could affect their safety
- how the quality of your services and products affects them
- about their methods of working
- how the timing of your work activities affects them
- how the sequencing of your work activities affects them
- what causes bottlenecks

You may have to adjust your work to effectively contribute to improving job and corporate performance.

Tell other workers how their work affects you. If their work affects your safety or productivity, you may have to adjust your ways of working or you may have to discuss the specific issues with them so that they make adjustments to their work to help you.

LEARNING ACTIVITY 19

Identify the impact of work on others

Effective coordination of work between workers and between departments is essential for maximizing job performance. Poor coordination between workers and work groups can create inefficiencies and hazardous situations. This learning activity focuses on ways your work affects others and how other workers can affect your ability to work effectively and efficiently.

19a. Identify a work assignment in which you must coordinate your activities with a co-worker. What could the consequences be if there is poor coordination?

_____

_____

_____

_____

19b. Identify a work project in which your activities must be coordinated with other specialized work groups. What could the consequences be if there is poor coordination between you and the work groups?

_____

_____

_____

_____

19c. Identify a project in which there is a need for coordination between different departments. What could the consequences be if there is poor coordination between departments?

_____

_____

19d. Identify a work project in which you must share tools or equipment with other workers or work groups. What could the consequences be if there is poor coordination of the use of tools and equipment?

_____

_____

_____

_____

19e. Identify a way of doing your work or project more efficiently. How could this change affect other workers, work groups, customers, and the technology?

_____

_____

_____

_____

19f. Give an example of a situation where you made an adjustment to your work to minimize the impact on others doing their work.

_____

_____

_____

_____

19g. Give an example of a situation where others made an adjustment to their work processes to minimize the impact on you doing your work.

_____

_____

_____

_____

Critical Thinking Questions

- How does my work affect other workers?
- How does my work affect other departments?
- How can I best coordinate my work with others?
- How do other workers affect my work?
- How do other departments affect my work?
- What should I do if other departments have a negative impact on my work?

Section 7

Thinking about Work

Contributing to job and corporate performance requires that you do your job competently while keeping the big picture in mind. You need to focus your efforts in ways that optimize the use of assets and minimize losses. You also need to continually look for ways to improve job and corporate performance. As part of contributing to your job and your organization, you must:

- work safely
- work effectively and efficiently
- use tools and equipment effectively
- work to extend the reliability and life of equipment
- ensure product quality
- minimize waste of materials
- protect the environment
- keep internal and external customers satisfied

Internal customers

Individuals, groups, or departments within an organization that provide services to other individuals, groups, or departments within the same organization:

- warehousing provides components and materials to maintenance department

---

(continued)

- maintenance department keeps equipment operating effectively for operating department
- operating department stops, isolates, and starts equipment for maintenance
- engineers modify equipment for operating and maintenance departments
- gas plant provides feed stock to another plant owned by the same company

You must also think through your work to optimize the use of assets and minimize losses by:
- understanding the reasons the work and technical processes are the way they are
- determining the cause(s) for changes in work and technical processes
- understanding the implications and consequences of changing work and technical processes and conditions
- responding effectively to changes in work and technical processes
- identifying conditions, actions, or events that can lead to a loss and taking action before a downgrading situation develops
- solving problems

To meet these expectations, you need a considerable amount of knowledge about your job, work and technical processes, organization, and its customers (internal and external). Because of the vast amount of knowledge that is available, you have to identify the critical knowledge that will benefit your work. For example, you could acquire detailed technical knowledge about a piece of equipment:
- how the equipment operates
- how to operate the equipment
- the equipment's design specifications

A valuable question to ask yourself is, *What do I need to know to be effective in the workplace?* Useful and practical knowledge is job focused and helps you to:
- perform your tasks at an exemplary level
- effectively carry out complex procedures

- optimize work and technical processes
- recognize abnormal conditions and possible consequences
- respond effectively to abnormal conditions
- solve problems
- make decisions in the best interest of your organization

Most organizations have site-specific and job-specific documentation, such as:
- safety manuals
- standards and procedures
- training manuals
- operating manuals
- maintenance manuals
- vendor literature
- engineering documents
- construction documents

From these internal documents, you can often gain the critical knowledge you need for your job. Understanding the *concepts, reasons, causes,* and *consequences* about equipment, materials, work processes, and technical processes can be very valuable in performing your work safely, effectively, and efficiently. You can also use the knowledge to respond to abnormal conditions and solve work problems.

LEARNING ACTIVITY 20

Optimize technical and work processes and minimize losses

You have an important part to play in contributing to job and corporate performance. Within your area of work, you need to work in ways that optimize technical and work processes and minimize losses. This learning activity helps you identify ways to meet your responsibility to work effectively and efficiently and to minimize losses.

20a. Select either a technical or work process associated with your area of work. Identify either a critical adjustment or critical step to a procedure.

State the technical or work process: _____

_____

State the critical adjustment or critical step to the procedure: _____

_____

State why the adjustment or step is critical: _____

_____

State how to execute the adjustment or step effectively:

_____

_____

_____

20b. Identify a change or abnormal condition that can lead to a downgrading incident: _____

_____

_____

State the potential consequences of the change or abnormal condition: _____

_____

_____

Identify the cause for the change or abnormal condition:

_____

_____

State what can be done, if anything, to prevent the change or abnormal condition from occurring: _____

_____

_____

If the change or abnormal condition occurs, describe your response to minimize the consequences: _____

_____

Critical Thinking Questions

- Why does the equipment operate this way?

- Why is this operational or maintenance task done this way?

- What could cause a change in equipment operation or condition?

- What are the consequences if there is a change in equipment operation or condition?

- How would I recognize a change in equipment operation or condition?

- How should I respond to a change in equipment operation or condition?

- What would be the consequences for PEMEO if I do not perform this step properly?

- What should I do if the results of performing this step are not as expected?

- How can I do this task more safely, effectively, efficiently, and with less effort?

JobThink™

Section 8

Solving Problems

Many day-to-day work problems need to be resolved immediately or within a couple of days. To effectively contribute to job and corporate performance, you need to be able to recognize work-related problems and take action within your roles and responsibilities.

Many different conditions, actions, or events can cause work-related problems, for example:
- staff shortages
- operating and maintenance mistakes
- delivery of wrong materials and components
- unsatisfactory equipment condition and/or function
- stationary and mobile equipment failure
- fluid leaks and spills from containers, vessels, piping, and equipment
- very large customer orders
- unexpected increase in customer orders
- inclement weather

But, not all conditions, actions, or events cause problems. A problem only exists when undesirable *consequences* to one or more domains of PEMEO are created, for example:

People	• harm to the health and safety of workers and the public • reduced worker productivity
Equipment	• degraded equipment condition and life • damage to equipment and facilities
Materials	• wasted materials • defective materials
Environment	• harm to the environment
Organization	• dissatisfied customers • lost production • damaged public image

Often, a condition, action, or event that causes a negative consequence for one PEMEO domain also causes negative consequences for other PEMEO domains. For example, a hazardous chemical spill can affect worker safety, damage equipment and materials, harm the environment, and cause a financial loss to the organization to clean up the spill, replenish the chemical, and pay the fines.

After you have identified a problem that falls within your roles and responsibilities, you need to take action to solve the problem (i.e., eliminate the cause and/or limit the undesired consequences). You also need to monitor the results of your actions to ensure the problem is solved effectively.

```
 ┌─ PROBLEM ──────┐
 │                │
 │  ┌──────────┐  │
 │  │ cause    │  │
 │  │ - condition │          ┌────────────┐      ┌──────────┐
 │  │ - action │  │─ ─ ─ ─   │ solution(s)│ ───▶ │  action  │
 │  │ - event  │  │          └────────────┘      └──────────┘
 │  └──────────┘  │                 ▲                  │
 │                │                 │                  ▼
 │  ┌──────────┐  │          ┌────────────┐
 │  │ undesired │ │─ ─ ─ ─   │  evaluate  │
 │  │ consequences │         │  results   │
 │  │ - PEMEO  │  │          └────────────┘
 │  └──────────┘  │
 └────────────────┘
```

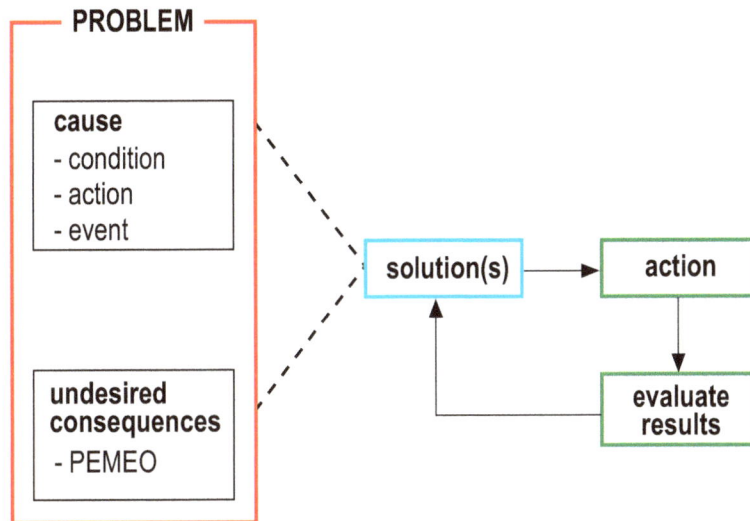

Sometimes solving a problem is difficult because:

- the root cause of the problem is difficult to define
- there may be more than one cause
- the undesired consequences of **not** resolving the problem are not well understood
- the criteria for selecting solutions are not specified
- there are too many solutions from which to choose
- the preferred solution is difficult to implement
- there is a lack of monitoring to ensure the corrective action is effective and does not have other undesirable consequences

The following **problem-solving model** is useful for many day-to-day work problems. More sophisticated or situation-specific problem solving and troubleshooting models may be required for complex technical and work process problems.

The following illustration provides an overview of the six steps you can use to solve problems. The rest of this section provides a detailed explanation of each problem-solving step.

PROBLEM SOLVING MODEL

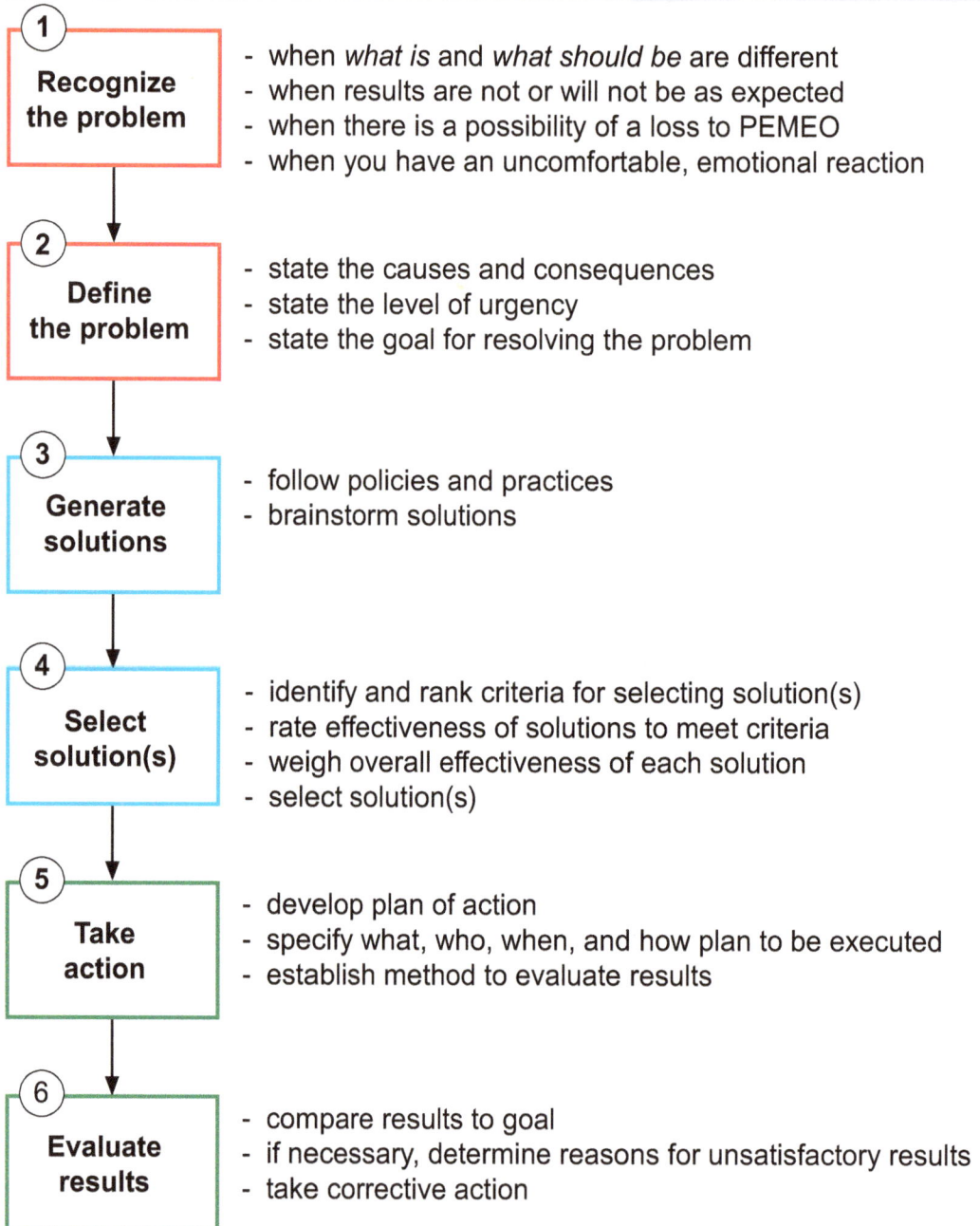

1 Recognize the problem
- when *what is* and *what should be* are different
- when results are not or will not be as expected
- when there is a possibility of a loss to PEMEO
- when you have an uncomfortable, emotional reaction

2 Define the problem
- state the causes and consequences
- state the level of urgency
- state the goal for resolving the problem

3 Generate solutions
- follow policies and practices
- brainstorm solutions

4 Select solution(s)
- identify and rank criteria for selecting solution(s)
- rate effectiveness of solutions to meet criteria
- weigh overall effectiveness of each solution
- select solution(s)

5 Take action
- develop plan of action
- specify what, who, when, and how plan to be executed
- establish method to evaluate results

6 Evaluate results
- compare results to goal
- if necessary, determine reasons for unsatisfactory results
- take corrective action

Step 1—Recognize the Problem

Many work-related problems are caused by conditions, actions, or events. A condition, action, or event causes a problem if undesirable consequences for the job and business are created, for example:

- when *what is* and *what should be* are different
- when results are not or will not be as expected (quantity, quality, time, timeliness, duration)
- when there is or could be a loss to PEMEO
- when you have an uncomfortable emotional reaction

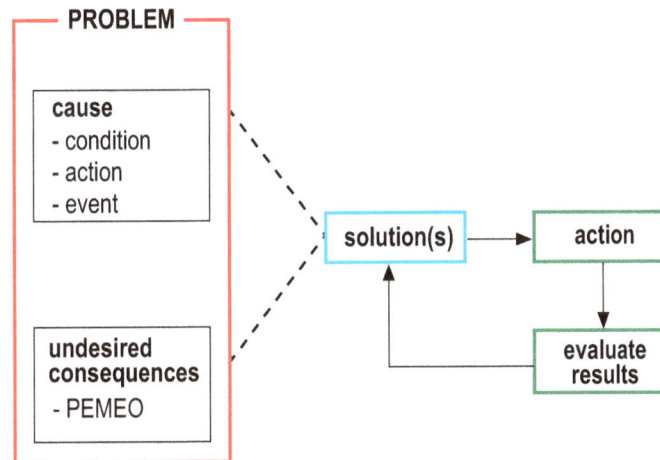

Ask yourself questions about the impact of the conditions, actions, or events on PEMEO, for example:

People	• Are workers or the public at risk?
	• Will worker productivity be reduced?
Equipment	• Could equipment be damaged?
	• Could equipment reliability be reduced?
Materials	• Will materials be wasted?
	• Is product quality substandard?
Environment	• Could the environment be contaminated?
Organization	• Will production schedules be affected?
	• Will there be a loss of production?
	• Will customers be dissatisfied?
	• Are there unplanned costs?
	• Will the product have to be recalled?
	• Could a regulatory infraction occur?

The following table provides some examples of conditions, actions, or events that can create undesirable consequences:

Condition, Action, or Event	Impact on PEMEO
The guardrail is loose.	Workers are at risk of falling.
The truck carrying gasoline drives off the road. The gasoline in the tank could leak.	The driver and public are at risk of injury and the environment could be contaminated.
The manufacturer substitutes the original materials of some components with materials that have less strength.	The equipment could fail prematurely.
The engine is running very hot.	The engine could be damaged.
The raw materials contain pieces of metal.	Process equipment could be damaged.
One production line station is two people short.	Production is bottlenecked, reducing throughput.
A crawler tractor is working in very tight quarters.	Major damage could occur to adjacent installations.
A customer places a very large order that has to be filled quickly.	Other customers will experience order shortages and delivery delays.
One group of trades people is not available as scheduled.	The completion date for the project could be delayed.

Sometimes the problem is created by a sequence of conditions, actions, or events such that:

- the *immediate* cause may not be the root cause. For example, a bearing failed (immediate cause), shutting down the equipment. The bearing failed because the wrong oil was used (root cause).
- the *immediate* consequences may not be the *measurable* consequences. For example, the hose carrying diesel fuel broke, spraying diesel fuel onto a hot furnace. The diesel fuel caught fire (immediate consequence). The furnace was damaged, causing a stoppage of production and expensive repairs (measurable consequences).

You may need to deal with the immediate cause and immediate consequences first to minimize the undesirable consequences for PEMEO. Determining the root causes and measuring the consequences may require considerable analysis and a lot more time.

Step 2—Define the Problem

After you have identified the problem, you must clearly define the problem so that the solution you choose is effective. To clearly define the problem:

- state the cause(s) and undesirable consequence(s)
- state the level of urgency
- state the goal for resolving the problem

State the causes and consequences

Examples of stating causes and consequences are provided in Step 1. Ask the 5W&H (Who? What? Where? When? Why? and How?) questions to further clarify the conditions, actions, events, and consequences (see examples below). Sometimes asking the 5W&H questions will also identify possible solutions.

5W&H Questions	Example Questions
Who?	• Who is involved in creating the condition, action, or event? • Who is affected? • Who is at risk of getting sick or injured?
What?	• What went wrong? • What caused the condition, action, or event? • What equipment and materials are involved? • What work processes are involved? • What damage has occurred or could occur to equipment, materials, and facilities? • What environmental impacts have or could occur? • What was the first response to the condition, action, or event? • What could have been done to prevent the problem from occurring?

(continued)

5W&H Questions	Example Questions
Where?	• Where did the incident take place? • Where were others when the incident took place?
When?	• When did the problem/incident occur? • When was the problem identified? • When did the first action take place to rectify he cause or limit the impacts to PEMEO? • When were key people informed?
Why?	• Why did the problem/incident occur? • Why didn't anyone take action in response to the problem? • Why did he or she take that specific action in response to the problem?
How?	• How did it happen? • How can the consequences be minimized? • How can the problem be prevented, eliminated, or controlled?

State the level of urgency

Problems differ in the amount of attention and effort they demand. Some problems may require the involvement of all levels of management and large budgets; other problems can be solved at the job level with minimal costs. One way to determine which problems you should deal with is to apply the concept of urgency.

The level of urgency for taking action is determined by:
• the PEMEO domain affected
• the severity of the consequence
• the need to prevent either undesired consequences from occurring or the severity of consequences from escalating

For example:
• which PEMEO domains are or could be affected? For example, an oil spill into a lake will:
  – affect tourism and the local drinking water supply (people)

- affect turbines at a downstream power station (equipment)
- affect wildlife (environment)
- be expensive to clean up and will damage the company's reputation (organization)

- the severity (magnitude, amount) of the consequences (e.g., a fire in the stock pile of lumber will cause extensive damage)
- the potential for the consequences to continue (e.g., one quarter of all pieces cut by machine were outside the tolerances for dimension)
- the potential of preventing the consequences (e.g., a container being filled with a fluid is about to overflow)
- the potential for the consequences to escalate (e.g., water begins to leak from a containment dike; the flow rate will increase quickly over time)
- the possibility of limiting the extent of the consequences (e.g., oil spilled into a lake will spread unless it is contained)
- the potential for the incident to reoccur (e.g., in the past week, the computer server crashed four times; the winch brake slipped twice under heavy load)

For many organizations, the two PEMEO domains of highest priority are people (safety) and environment. For these organizations, taking action when safety or the environment are at risk is more urgent than when other domains (equipment, materials, and organization) are at risk. Each organization ranks the importance of the PEMEO domains differently. Generally, the lower the ranking of a PEMEO domain, the less urgent the response, but the level of urgency increases when the level of severity to any domain increases.

To determine the level of urgency, make a table such as the one on the next page:
- list and rank the PEMEO domains according to your organization's priorities
- for each domain, list specific consequences
- for each specific category, state the level of severity of consequence

In the following example of determining the urgency to a specific incident, note that specific consequences are identified and then ranked for importance within the domain. Five levels of severity for consequences (none, low, moderate, high, extreme) are used. If there is no undesirable consequence for a domain, place **None** in the severity column to indicate that the domain was considered.

Ranked Domain	Specific Consequences	Severity of Consequences
People	safety of workers and public	moderate
Environment	damage to environment	low
	regulatory infraction	none
Equipment	damage to equipment	low
	reduced equipment reliability	low
Materials	loss of materials	extreme
Organization	loss of production	moderate
	unplanned costs	moderate
	dissatisfied customers	high
	disruption to public	low

NOTE

Many organizations require *urgent action* if there is danger to workers and the public or potential for damage to the environment, even if the level of severity is low. In the table above, **People** and **Environment** are written in bold type to indicate that the problem is urgent if either or both these domains are affected.

Consider the following criteria when determining the level of severity:
- danger to workers and the public
- damage to the environment
- the ranking of the domain for importance. The higher the domain ranking, the more urgent it is to take action.
- the severity (or potential severity) of consequences.

Generally, the more severe the consequence, the more urgent it is to take action. However, just because a domain has severe consequences, it does not automatically mean that the problem is urgent. For a low ranked domain, the organization may not consider the problem urgent, even if the consequences are severe (e.g., a piece of equipment fails, but the equipment is not often used or is scheduled to be replaced).

In addition to domain and severity of consequences, two other factors must be considered when determining the level of urgency:
• preventing undesired consequences from occurring
• preventing the severity of consequences from escalating

Some conditions, actions, or events may not create an immediate problem, but if action is not taken quickly, undesired consequences will occur. Some consequences will become more severe if immediate action is not taken. In the table on the previous page, review your ratings of severity and increase the rating for those consequences that will be created or will become more severe if the problem is not dealt with soon.

The level of urgency to take action is based on the ranking of the domain and on the severity of consequences. Taking into account Domain rank and severity of consequences, select the three or four **Consequences** that are the most urgent for taking action (short list). Here is an example from the above list:
• safety of workers and the public
• damage to the environment
• loss of materials
• dissatisfied customers

The short list makes it easier to identify and select solutions. Identifying the consequences that have a high level of severity can also be useful in determining appropriate solutions where the goal is to minimize impact.

Other consequences are important to the organization but there is less urgency in finding solutions. And often, solutions to a problem that address the most urgent consequences will also address the less urgent consequences (e.g., repairing damaged equipment can also improve equipment reliability).

State the goal

The goal for resolving the problem may be to:
- eliminate the cause of the problem
- minimize the impact of the problem
- prevent the problem from recurring

Often the goal is the flip side of the problem (cause or consequence). For example:
- the cause of the problem is that the engine failed. The goal is to get the engine operating within four hours.
- the consequences of the problem are that productivity is reduced and customers will be dissatisfied. The goals are to:
  - increase productivity by 20 items per day within the next 48 hours, and
  - inform customers of the delays and the actions that will be taken to minimize the impact on them

In these examples, measurable results (e.g., 4 hours, 20 items, 48 hours) are stated so that you can determine if the actions you will be taking to resolve the problem are effective.

Many day-to-day work problems are temporarily solved by implementing short-term solutions to minimize the consequences. Sometimes actions may also be taken to prevent the problem from recurring. Implementing a permanent solution may require extensive planning and a significant budget.

Step 3—Generate Solutions

Your organization may have specific response plans, policies, or procedures for responding to some specific types of problem. These plans, policies, or procedures may vary from one application or circumstance to another. For example, pipelines transporting liquid petroleum products can leak, endangering the public and the environment. The required response to a potential leak may vary for different pipelines and companies. For example, depending on the company and pipeline, the pipeline control center operator may be required to do one of the following:

- if there is a possibility of a leak, shut down the pipeline and then investigate
- investigate and then, if there is a possibility of a leak, shut down the pipeline
- notify others about a potential leak but do not shut down the pipeline. Shutting down the pipeline without adequate notice to suppliers could cause other serious problems.

When applying your organization's plans, policies, and procedures to solve a problem, make sure that the prescribed response is the correct one for the situation.

For problems that do not have prescribed solutions, you and others may have to determine the best action to take. First, list possible solutions to the problem and then select the solution(s) that will be most effective. Use the brainstorming technique to generate possible solutions. In a brainstorming session:

- Have group members identify as many solutions as possible. Do not debate or discuss the value of the suggestions. The goal is to identify as many solutions as possible.
- When it becomes difficult to think of additional solutions, stop the brainstorming and select the solutions that seem plausible. Do not assume that solutions used in the past to solve the same or similar problem will be effective for this situation; circumstances can change.
- Sometimes two or more solutions can be combined to solve a problem. For example, to deal with staff shortages, temporary help could be used and/or the hours of work extended. To determine which solutions may be plausible, do a brief assessment of each solution. This assessment helps eliminate solutions that are not plausible and is also useful for selecting the best solutions (Step 4).
- To assess each solution, determine:
  - what has to be done
  - required resources such as equipment, parts, materials, and people

- availability of resources
- how long it will take to implement the solution. Usually, the longer it takes to implement a solution, the greater the accumulated loss to the organization.
- the cost to implement the solution. Some solutions may be costly but essential for meeting critical corporate objectives. The cost of not solving the problem may quickly become much higher than the cost of implementing the solution. Some solutions may be implemented at very little cost. Temporarily changing work processes may not have a noticeable cost. For example, an outside wall for a house under construction cannot be erected safely because of the wind. One possible solution is to build other outside walls while waiting for the wind to subside.
- the effectiveness of the solution(s) to solve the problem. The focus of solutions can be on eliminating the cause, on limiting or eliminating the consequences, or on preventing the problem from reoccurring. Some solutions may only address some of the undesired consequences identified in Step 2. For example, a solution may address equipment damage but does not address customer dissatisfaction.

Step 4—Select Solutions

You need criteria to select the best solution(s) for the problem, Criteria for making a selection include:

- effectiveness in solving the problem (i.e., achieving the goals identified in Step 2)
- time required to implement the solution
- resources required to implement the solution
- availability of resources
- cost of the solution

Add any selection criteria that are specific to the job and business. For example, an outside agency may have to give approval before implementing the solution. If possible, delete criteria that are unimportant or are not applicable so that decision-making is easier. For example, if all the necessary resources are readily available, *availability of resources* can be eliminated from the list. Identify the criteria (e.g., safety) that **must** be addressed.

If there are only a few criteria and/or solutions or one obviously superior solution, you can mentally make the assessment and select the best solution. However, make sure that the critical criteria, such as safety and environment, are effectively addressed.

A matrix can help you be more thorough at assessing and selecting solutions. In the following illustration, the selection criteria are *ranked* in order of priority in the left column. The critical criteria that **must** be addressed are in bold. Possible solutions are listed in the row along the top of the matrix.

Selection Criteria (ranked)	Rating of Possible Solutions		
	Solution 1	Solution 2	Solution 3
safety			
environment			
materials			
customers			
time			
resources			
availability of resources			
cost			

In the example below, a scale of 0 to 5 is used to rate how effectively each solution addresses each criterion—5 being the best because it fully addresses the criterion and 0 indicating that the solution does not address the criterion.

To rate the solutions, review the information about the solutions you recorded in Step 3. You may have to gather additional information for some criterion you have identified in Step 4.

Selection Criteria (ranked)	Rating of Possible Solutions		
	Solution 1	Solution 2	Solution 3
safety	5	5	0
environment	5	0	5
materials	3	4	3
customers	5	4	4
time	3	4	4
resources	2	5	3
availability of resources	5	5	3
cost	3	5	5

Solution 1 is the only solution that addresses both safety and environment, the two criteria that **must** be addressed. However, you could combine solutions 2 and 3 so that both safety and environment are addressed. Compare the details (e.g., cost) of each solution to help you determine the best solution(s).

If it is difficult to decide which solution is best, you can use a more rigorous arithmetical approach.

1. Assign a number (weighting factor) from 1 to 10 to each selection criterion to rank the importance of that criterion to achieving the goal (refer to the table that follows). Care must be given when assigning a weighting factor. A small change can dramatically affect which solution is considered the best.

2. For each solution, assign a number from 0 to 5 to rate how effectively each solution addresses the selection criterion. Note that, in the table below, the rating numbers from the previous example are used.

Selection Criteria (ranked)	Weighting Factor	Rating of Possible Solutions		
		Solution 1	Solution 2	Solution 3
safety	10	5	5	0
environment	10	5	0	5
materials	7	3	4	3
customers	7	5	4	4
time	6	3	4	4
resources	4	2	5	3
availability of resources	4	5	5	3
cost	2	3	5	5

3. For each solution, multiply the weighting factor by the rating number to determine the overall contribution of the solution to achieving the goal (see Solution 1 in the example below).

Selection Criteria (ranked)	Weighting Factor	Rating of Possible Solutions		
		Solution 1	Solution 2	Solution 3
safety	10	10 x 5 = 50	50	0
environment	10	50	0	50
materials	7	21	28	21
customers	7	35	28	28
time	6	18	24	24
resources	4	8	20	12
availability of resources	4	20	20	12
cost	2	6	10	10
		208	**180**	**157**

Total the numbers for each solution. The solution with the highest total is considered the best solution. If you have an uncomfortable feeling about the results, review the weighting factors for the selection criteria and the rating numbers for the solutions. Any changes you make to the numbers could change the results. Also, take into account that the solutions address the most urgent concerns; other solutions may be required to address less urgent concerns.

IMPORTANT

After you have selected the solution(s), check to determine if the solution(s) can have an undesirable effect on other areas of the organization (PEMEO).

Step 5—Take Action

Many day-to-day solutions can be implemented without creating a formal plan of action. For complex solutions, however, a plan of action must be developed that takes into account worker roles, responsibilities, and authority. A plan of action specifies, as a minimum:

- *what* action must be taken
- *who* will carry out the action
- *when* the action will be carried out or completed
- *how* the results of the action will be monitored to determine the effectiveness of the solution in achieving the goal

The plan of action may be developed by one or more individuals. Experts from outside the organization may have to be included in the group developing the plan. The first step is to identify the major activities that must take place (as shown in the example below). Then determine the *who* and the *when*. The *who* may include third-party *personnel*. The *when* can include the start and/or finish times. *How* to carry out the activities may be determined by the worker who is assigned to do the work or by the group involved in the planning.

What (activity)	Who	When
Shut down and isolate equipment		
Clean up area		
Order parts		
Inform customers		
Adjust shipments		
Repair equipment		
Start up equipment		
Fill back orders		
Evaluate results		

Someone should be assigned to monitor the progress in implementing the plan. If difficulties arise in executing the plan, that person can either take action or have the group meet to change the plan or resolve the difficulties.

Step 6—Evaluate Results

In Step 2 of this problem-solving model, the stated goal included measurable results. The person assigned to evaluate the results of taking action to resolve the problem compares the actual results with the desired results. For more complex problems, the assessment can also determine if:

- the most urgent criteria have been met
- the less urgent criteria have been met
- the action plan was carried out effectively

If the results are unsatisfactory, investigate to determine the reasons for the goals not being achieved. The problem-solving process may have to be repeated (starting at Step 3, Generate Solutions) to address specific issues.

LEARNING ACTIVITY 21

Solve work-related problems

Responding effectively to work-related problems is an important part of contributing to job and corporate performance. This learning activity helps you apply the problem-solving model to a workplace problem you may have. For each step of this learning activity, refer to the written explanations on previous pages.

Step 1: Recognize the problem

1a. Identify a work-related problem for which there are several possible solutions.

Problem _____

_____

1b. Identify the conditions, actions, or events that caused the problem.

_____

_____

_____

1c. Identify the current or future impact that the conditions, actions, or events have on PEMEO.

Domain	Impact
People	• • •
Equipment	• • •
Materials	• • •

(continued)

Domain	Impact
Environment	• • •
Organization	• • •

Step 2: Define the problem

2a.   Ask the 5W&H questions to clarify the causes and consequences of the problem.

5W&H	Example Questions
Who?	• • •
What?	• • •
Where?	• • •
When?	• • •
Why?	• • •
How?	• • •

2b. Specify the PEMEO domains that are affected by the problem. Be specific.

_____

_____

_____

_____

_____

_____

_____

_____

2c. In the table below, rank the PEMEO domains from the most important to the least important (from your organization's point of view). For each domain, list the specific consequences.

Ranked Domain	Specific Consequences	Severity of Consequences

2d. From the table you developed in 2c, select the four domains which are the most urgent for taking action.

_____

_____

_____

_____

2e. State the goal, including measurable results, for resolving the problem.

_____

_____

_____

Step 3: Generate solutions

3a. Does your organization have policies and practices stating the required response to the problem? If yes, state the policies and practices.

_____

_____

_____

_____

_____

3b. List some possible solutions to the problem.

_____

_____

_____

_____

_____

_____

_____

3c. Select three solutions. For each solution, fill in the information required in the following table.

Solution 1: _____

What has to be done	
Required resources	
Availability of resources	
Time needed to implement solution	
Costs	
Effectiveness in resolving the problem (very, quite, somewhat)	

Solution 2: _____

What has to be done	
Required resources	
Availability of resources	
Time needed to implement solution	
Costs	
Effectiveness in resolving the problem (very, quite, somewhat)	

Solution 3: _____

What has to be done	
Required resources	
Availability of resources	
Time needed to implement solution	
Costs	
Effectiveness in resolving the problem (very, quite, somewhat)	

Step 4: Select solution(s)

4a. Complete the following table:

1. Identify and rank the criteria for selecting solutions.

2. Identify criteria that must be addressed (e.g., safety).

3. Rate each solution on a scale of 5 to 0 for its effectiveness in addressing each criterion (5 is very effective and 0 does not address the criterion).

Selection Criteria (ranked)	Rating of Possible Solutions		
	Solution 1	Solution 2	Solution 3

4b. The best solution(s) for resolving the problem is (are):

_____

_____

_____

Step 5: Take action

5.   Develop a plan of action by filling out the table below. Make the last entry *Evaluate results*.

What (activity)	Who	When

Step 6:   Evaluate results

6a. How would you monitor the execution of the action plan?

_____

_____

_____

6b. How would you know the problem has been resolved effectively?

_____

_____

_____

Critical Thinking Questions

- What exactly is the problem?
- What conditions, actions, or events created the problem?
- What are the potential consequences of the problem?
- Is this problem urgent enough to take action?
- Is there a prescribed response to the problem?
- What are the possible solutions to resolve the problem?
- What is the best solution to resolve the problem?
- What is the plan of action to resolve the problem?
- How do I know the problem has been resolved satisfactorily?

JobThink™

Job Aid

Critical Thinking Questions

Constituents of an Organization

- What are the beliefs and values of my organization?
- What are my roles and responsibilities?
- Who are my internal and external customers?
- What are my limits of authority?
- What is the management style of this department?
- What are my department's goals for the year?
- How does my work contribute to achieving department goals?
- How does the quality of my work impact the organization?
- What corporate objectives are important to my department?

Relationship between Constituents

- What quality of equipment does this organization use?
- What is my organization's strategy for maintaining equipment?
- What equipment must operate reliably?
- How can I contribute to the reliability of equipment?
- How can I extend the life of equipment?
- How do I report damaged equipment?
- What are the most important tasks?
- What are the most important aspects of this task?

Resources

- What are the critical cost-related issues of my job?
- What equipment do I need to do this job safely, effectively, and efficiently?
- How can I make the best use of materials?
- What am I supposed to do with waste?
- How can I protect the environment?
- How are decisions made regarding change?
- What tasks are considered critical?
- Can I decide on my own how to do the work?
- What policies and practices are important to doing my work?
- How do I know I am doing the tasks satisfactorily?
- How can I work more safely, effectively, and efficiently?
- What job-specific training does the organization provide?

Strategic Business Objectives

- What are my organization's strategic business objectives?
- What are the benchmarks for the SBOs?
- What strategies does the organization use to achieve the SBOs?
- How can I contribute to achieving the SBOs?

Impact of Work on Other Workers

- How does my work affect other workers?
- How does my work affect other departments?
- How can I best coordinate my work with others?
- How do other workers affect my work?
- How do other departments affect my work?
- What should I do if other departments have a negative impact on my work?

Thinking about Work

- Why does the equipment operate this way?
- Why is this operational or maintenance task done this way?
- What could cause a change in equipment operation or condition?
- What are the consequences if there is a change in equipment operation or condition?
- How would I recognize a change in equipment operation or condition?
- How should I respond to a change in equipment operation or condition?
- What would be the consequences for PEMEO if I do not perform this step properly?
- What should I do if the results of performing this step are not as expected?
- How can I do this task more safely, effectively, efficiently, and with less effort?

Solving Problems

- What exactly is the problem?
- What conditions, actions, or events created the problem?
- What are the potential consequences of the problem?
- Is this problem urgent enough to take action?
- Is there a prescribed response to the problem?
- What are the possible solutions to resolve the problem?
- What is the best solution to resolve the problem?
- What is the plan of action to resolve the problem?
- How do I know the problem has been resolved satisfactorily?

Another book by Gordon D. Shand

Interviewing to Gather Relevant Content for Training

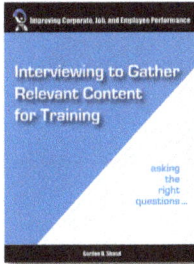

Effective training contributes to business success—**improved corporate, job, and employee performance**. But how do you figure out what training is effective? This book provides the strategies you need to identify training that will give you the best return on your investment in training.

Part A:
- provides criteria and strategies you can use to identify:
  - training content that is relevant
  - what content you should address and not address
- describes pitfalls that you can encounter and ways to resolve these pitfalls

Part B describes an interviewing process where you provide leadership to identify and gather content that is relevant, useful, and practical. You will learn how to:
- help the subject matter expert provide quality content
- select content that is relevant and eliminate content that will not improve performance
- keep the subject matter expert engaged
- structure the content to effectively and efficiently develop training and assessment resources

The suggestions in this book are the accumulated experiences of many training and performance consultants who have encountered the challenges of gathering relevant content and developing effective training.

Who can benefit?

- educational, training, and performance consultants
- training program designers
- instructional designers
- technical writers
- trainers and coaches
- internal staff who develop training

www.ingramcontent.com/pod-product-compliance
Lightning Source LLC
Chambersburg PA
CBHW050240220326
41598CB00047B/7459